.. The ..
. 38th BATTALION .
A. I. F.

.. The ..
Story and Official History
of the
38th Battalion A. I. F.

... By ERIC FAIREY ...

Foreword by Rt. Hon. W. M. HUGHES,
Prime Minister of Australia.

—ILLUSTRATED—

The Naval & Military Press Ltd

Published by
The Naval & Military Press Ltd
5 Riverside, Brambleside, Bellbrook
Industrial Estate, Uckfield, East Sussex,
TN22 1QQ England
Tel: +44 (0) 1825 749494
Fax: +44 (0) 1825 765701
www.naval-military-press.com
www.military-genealogy.com
www.militarymaproom.com

Printed and bound in Great Britain by
CPI Antony Rowe, Chippenham and Eastbourne
*In reprinting in facsimile from the original, any imperfections are inevitably reproduced
and the quality may fall short of modern type and cartographic standards.*

Dedicated to our Fallen, who gave their all in the service of their Country.

When the sunset has burnt out its flare in the west
    For the footsteps of sweet, dusky Night,
There's an angel who bends over Mother Earth's breast
    Where his little cross stands lone and white.

And the gay poppies laugh at the touch of her brush
    Which was dipped in the sunset so red,
And is swept o'er the sky when the stars are a hush
    For blue cornflowers asleep on his bed.

When Morning awakes with a broad, sunny smile,
    The angel goes back to the saints
Who gathered Dawn's gold as she lingered awhile
    Near the flower-covered graves, which she paints.

                      —Author

: Foreword :

IT gives me very great pleasure, indeed, to write the foreword to the History of the 38th Battalion. The hearts of the people of Bendigo and District will surely be stirred when they read again of the glorious deeds of their own boys at Messines, Ypres, Passchendaele, and Amiens. The world has rung time and time again during the long years of war with the deeds of the A.I.F., and we, as Australians, have been proud to call them brothers. But it is especially gratifying for the people of Bendigo to know that their sons were present and distinguished themselves in those great battles, the memory of which will endure as long as time itself.

The darkest days of our apparent defeat were brightened by their glorious deeds of valour. In the stopping of the enemy before Amiens, perhaps the most decisive period of the war, these 38th Battalion boys played a great part, and later, in that victorious onslaught on the Hindenburg line which swept the enemy's hordes before them, they were ever in the forefront.

Every Bendigo man should read this book and tell the glorious story to his children and their children's children. This history of the deathless deeds of the boys of the 38th Battalion should become like household words, familiar in the mouths of all who love Australia, and look to Bendigo and district as their home.

We are proud that they are Australians. We are particularly proud that so many are Bendigonians.

W. M. Hughes

Prime Minister of Australia.

:: ILLUSTRATIONS ::

I.—Strazeele: The Battalion's First Billets in France
II.—Half-past-Eleven Square, Armentieres
III.—Through Armentieres to the Front Line
IV.—Battalion Graves, Strand Cemetery, Ploegsteert
V.—Hill 63 and Ploegsteert Wood
VI.—Lille Gate, Ypres
VII.—A Big Crater at Ypres
VIII.—Flanders Mud
IX.—Gibraltar : A Typical Pill Box
XI.—Group of 38th Battalion Officers
     Aldershot Camp, Neuve Eglise
XII.—Group or 38th Battalion N.C.O.'s
     Aldershot Camp, Neuve Eglise
XIII.—The Edge of Marrett Wood
XIV.—Corbie Cathedral
XV.—Vaux Wood and the Road leading to Curlu
XVI.—The Somme River near Corbie
XVII.—38th Battalion Band, Hamilton Wood
XVIII.—" C " Company in Dog Trench
     Hindenburg Line

OFFICERS COMMANDING THE 38th BATTALION A.I.F.

Colonel C. H. DAVIS, C.B.E., D.S.O., V.D.

Lieut.-Col. G. HURRY, D.S.O.

The History
... of the ...
38th Battalion, A.I.F.

:: Chapter I. — Creating a Fighting Force. ::

The birthplace of the Thirty-eighth Battalion was in the Australian bush, three miles north-east of the City of Bendigo in the State of Victoria, where white tents stood out against a background of gumtrees from whose branches the kookaburra sounded a joyous reveille at the first streak of dawn, and the mopoke solemnly sounded the "Last Post" 'neath a jewel studded sky.

The training ground selected by the military authorities was an ideal one, for it embraced the Epsom Racecourse, a green carpet laid down amid summer-brown fields.

Among the shady gums, where the kookaburras lived, men hopped in and out of trenches, and cut such strange capers that the wise-looking old birds were wont to give expression to their feelings in occasional bursts of laughter.

And so, amid their own beloved bush, the men who had banded together in the cause of Freedom and Justice gathered new strength to face the hardships which they well knew the near future must bring.

The Battalion was formed on the first day of March, 1916, as one of the units of the Tenth Brigade, 3rd Division; Lieut.-Col. C. H. Davis being appointed to command.

On this day 201 other ranks were taken on strength as a nucleus. The work of forming a nucleus or a foundation upon which to build the Battalion, was very successfully carried out by Capt. L. L. Smith.

Training on the lines laid down by Administrative Headquarters was actively carried on, and with the addition of fresh drafts the Unit soon afterwards reached War Establishment. Despite the fact that most of the N.C.O.'s selected to instruct raw recruits were, unfortunately, withdrawn to schools, the task of moulding the men proceeded in a satisfactory manner, and in a few short weeks the C.O. could well feel proud of the men who "sloped arms" and marched with that easy grace only to be found in the movements of the well-trained soldier.

The days passed by very happily.

Bendigo held many attractions, for the citizens entertained men on leave with lavish hospitality. Many a soldier, a stranger to the Golden City, soon discovered true friends who made their house his home, and did all in their power to brighten the hours of leave. The ever-open doors of the Y.M.C.A. welcomed him, and on Sunday evenings this splendid Association invited him to gather round the appetising tea tables where the ladies of Bendigo presided and made him feel so thoroughly at home.

With the month of May came a disquieting interruption when a severe outbreak of cerebro-spinal meningitis was responsible for interfering with the work of training. All sorts of expedients were tried to arrest the persistent progress of the epidemic, until finally the whole Battalion was subjected to severe medical examination, and all those found thoroughly healthy were removed to Campbellfield on June 5th. These measures proving effective the training went on uninterruptedly and strength was made up with fresh drafts.

On 14th of June a most impressive ceremonial parade took place, and in the presence of a large number of friends and visitors, the King's and Regimental colors were presented, on behalf of the Citizens of Bendigo, by the Governor-General, Sir Ronald Munro Ferguson, K.C.M.G. The Battalion was drawn up in line, the colors cased, being in rear of the centre in charge of two Color-Sergeants. The Battalion then formed three sides of a square and drums were piled in the centre. The colors were consecrated by the Chaplain and the Commanding-Officer (Lieut.-Col. C. H. Davis) then handed the King's color to His Excellency the Governor-General, who presented it to the Senior Lieutenant, Lieut. F. E. Fairweather, who received it, sinking on the right knee.

The Second in Command, Major R. O. Henderson, then handed the Regimental Color to His Excellency and the Second Senior Lieutenant (Lieut. J. H. Moore) received it as above mentioned.

The Lieutenants then arose and the Governor-General addressed the Battalion ere the Colors were given a general salute.

Six days later the Battalion, the Tenth Field Engineers, and Tenth Field Ambulance bade farewell to Australia's sunny shores.

Tuesday, the 20th of June, 1916, will never be forgotten by those who sailed away, or by their relatives and friends who crowded the Port Melbourne pier to bid them a speedy and safe return. No. 54, H.M.A.T. Runic was draped with khaki, for the men swarmed up into the rigging, and occupied every vantage point of the vessel. From the pier hundreds of reels of colored paper ribbon were thrown aboard, and soon a wonderful network of color screened the drab hull of the Runic. Thousands of gay flags, scarfs and handkerchiefs gladdened a scene which could so easily have been a sad one.

When the transport moved slowly out from the pier it seemed that the fragile streamers reluctantly let the great liner go forth upon its danger-fraught way.

Snap! Snap!! Snap!!! The straining ribbons parted, and floated like colored seaweed on the blue waters of the Bay. Lovers wound them in, dripping and soiled, and tucked them away in peggy bags or tunic pockets. Parents, wives and sweethearts waved a last farewell, and eyes bravely smiled through a mist of tears, and strained to catch a last glimpse of a loved one until the vessel became a blurred mass of frantically waving figures.

And thus passed the S.S. Runic out to the blue Southern Ocean.

The following were the officers who embarked with the Unit:—

C.O.—Lieut.-Colonel C. H. Davis.
Second Command.—Major R. O. Henderson.
"A" Company.—Capt. G. V. Lansell, O.C.; Capt. R. E. Trebilcock; Lieut. F. E. Fairweather; Lieut. W. J. Collins; Lieut. W. L. Lipshut; 2nd Lieut.. C. H. Peters.

"B" Company.—Capt. L. L. Smith, O.C.; Capt. E. F. Moore, Lieut. E. W. Latchford, Lieut. H. Dench. 2nd Lieut. F. C. Morrison, 2nd Lieut. F. R. B. Martin.

"C" Company.—Major G. Hurry, O.C.; Capt. J. Ackeroyd, Lieut. R. D. Tyers, 2nd Lieut. H. McColl, 2nd Lieut. J. L. Whitehead, 2nd Lieut. W. Maxwell.

"D" Company.—Capt. A. J. A. Maudsley, O.C.; Capt. H. F. Selleck. Lieut. J. H. Moore, 2nd Lieut. W. L. Bogle, 2nd Lieut., A. L. Reid.

1st 38th Reinforcements.—Lieut. W. H. Orchard, Adjutant Capt. A. Fraser; Quartermaster, Capt. R. N. Marks; Chaplain, Capt. Rev. W. N. Gunson; Medical Officer, Capt. J. McCusker; Lewis Gun Officer, 2nd Lieut. J. B. O'Donnell.

Capetown, South Africa, was the first port of call, and the three weeks' voyage to the Cape was uneventful.

Life aboard a troopship can be very monotonous, but energetic people aboard the Runic constantly broke the monotony by arranging capital sports programmes and concerts which were so thoroughly enjoyed by all, and which helped to keep one physically fit and cheerful.

Except for a slight outbreak of measles and meningitis the health of the troops was good. Two deaths resulted from these diseases, which were quickly defeated by the 10th Field Ambulance. This Unit did a splendid work throughout the voyage to England.

Everybody was in fine spirits on the day that land was sighted; and when on entering Table Bay the world-famed mountain stood out in all its rugged grandeur, excitement ran high. Five days were spent at the Cape, during which time liberal leave was granted when the beauties of Camps Bay, Sea Point, the Lion's Head and many other delightful places were explored.

One of the finest motor trips in the world may be made at the Cape. A circular road runs around Table Mountain for over thirty miles. Leaving Capetown it winds its way for twelve miles along the sea coast at the foot of the Twelve Apostles (huge fantastic peaks which tower up into the heavens) and dips up and down along the rugged shore, where the league-long rollers dash against massive rocks, and fling white showers of spray to the sunshine.

Suddenly the road turns inland, and runs through Arcadian forests of oak and silver-leaf trees, and finally winds its way back to Capetown through the pine forests of Wynberg. Those who were fortunate enough to make this trip will never forget its wonderful variety of scenery. the wild grandeur of shores and mountains; the soft beauty of Arcadian-like avenues; the magnificent forests of pines, and, towering above all this loveliness the eternal mountain, and the tablecloth of clouds hanging over its flat summit.

On the second day of the stay at Capetown the Battalion marched through the town and out to the Cecil Rhodes monument. Passing through a native village thousands of dusky men, children and women showed great interest in the march. especially the children who straightway started a begging campaign for "tickeys," or threepenny bits.

On arrival at the monument, the Battalion was invited to lunch by the ladies of Capetown. This instance of kind hospitality was one of many which the Unit received during the stay at the Cape.

A fine body of native troops put in an appearance on the Capetown wharf ere the Runic sailed. These men were Jamaicans, and had just cleaned up the Germans in West Africa. They were huge, thick-set men. and wore their uniforms with an air of pride. They seemed to be thoroughly enjoying the game of war, spoke optimistically of the fighting that awaited them in East Africa, and hoped to see France at an early date.

On leaving the Cape rough weather was experienced for forty-eight hours, but the days that followed were calm and sunny. The nights were particularly enjoyable; the Southern Cross gleamed like a diamond pendant in the tropic sky, and the calm ocean glowed with phosphorus through which the vessel cut a pathway of fire.

Boat drill now became a daily event.

The decks would present a peaceful scene, men reading, playing games and lolling about in the warm sunshine. Then quite unexpected the practise submarine alarm would sound when everyone would snatch up life-belts and hasten to their posts.

It one day happened that the sailors accidentally dropped some heavy tackle across the syren lanyard, which caused the genuine submarine alarm (a long blast of the syren) to disturb the peace. Great excitement prevailed, but everyone took up their positions in a cool and orderly manner, and laughingly dispersed when it was discovered that the alarm was the result of an accident.

The days now grew unpleasantly hot, for King Neptune's coral palace was not far away, and on a wireless message arriving from His Submarine Majesty every arrangement was made to receive him. and to present a number of officers and men to the venerable monarch. A large canvas bath was rigged up on the main deck, and was eyed with mingled feelings.

A fanfare of trumpets finally announced the arrival of King Neptune and his Court.

A long tow beard gave the aged monarch a fatherly appearance, and a cardboard crown encircled a brow from which war failed to drive away a look of serenity. His charming daughter was the cynosure of all eyes. What soldier ever failed to admire a pretty girl? And this lovely maid had the blue of the ocean in her eyes; her wealth of tow tresses gleamed in the hot sunshine; while her every movement was the personification of regal beauty.

Dark-skinned police now commenced to arrest officers and men and drag them before a court of justice over which Father Neptune presided. The victims were awarded tasteful soap pills, and their faces lathered with paste which a large wooden razor partly removed ere they were dipped back into the briny bath and thoroughly washed by attendants. The fact that one might be faultlessly attired in tussore silk garments did not prevent him escaping the ordeal, as several people discovered.

Shortly after the royal visit warm tropical rains drifted across the ocean, and the air became heavy and oppressive. Life 'tween decks was unbearable, and on deck the incessant rain made things very uncomfortable.

St. Vincent, Cape Verde Islands, was reached on 2nd August. Excepting the novelty of once again beholding land the half day's stay did not prove a very interesting time, for leave ashore could not be granted on account of the unhealthy climate. Viewed from the Runic the town of St. Vincent appeared to be fairly large; fine buildings and residences peeped through the palms which graced the rocky shore. The scattered islands could hardly be called picturesque, although patches of tropical vegetation softened their rugged features. Native canoes swarmed about the troopship and watching the dusky islanders diving for pennies proved amusing entertainment.

After leaving the tropics the weather grew congenial. The last three days of the long voyage were flavored with a certain amount of excitement. The torpedo-boat destroyers which were to escort the Runic through the sub-marine-infected waters failed to put in an appearance. It was an anxious time for Captain Kearney, the ship's commander. The nights were moonlight, favoring submarine operations, and for forty-eight hours the Captain kept to the bridge, ready for any emergency.

England was sighted on the morning of the 10th August, and shortly after midday the Runic entered Devonport.

The Battalion disembarked at Plymouth at 2 p.m., and entrained for Lark Hill Camp, Salisbury Plains.

After long weeks at sea, the glorious Devon country delighted the eye. Summer in all her glory reigned in woods and fields. Cornfields stood out like blocks of gold against the green pasture lands where sheep and cattle peacefully browsed in the scented sunshine. League upon league of smiling country unfolded to the swift train, and its beauty was applauded by sea-weary men. At Exeter the Battalion was heartily welcomed by the citizens who crowded the railway platform, and served refreshments and cigarettes. This warm welcome to England was greatly appreciated by all, and rousing cheers were given for the good folk of Exeter when the train journey was resumed. Lark Hill was reached at midnight.

Next morning, the Battalion's new home was viewed with great interest. Thousands of huts dotted the undulating country for miles around. The picturesque village of Amesbury nestled in a green hollow below the camp, and its old ivy-covered church and quaint gabled houses seemed to slumber to the droning of the bees in the flower-filled gardens. The village became a popular place of recreation, for entertainment was provided at a large Y.M.C.A. hut, and at a cinema.

The camp accommodation was good, hot and cold shower baths, ablution huts, and conveniences for washing clothes making conditions reasonably comfortable.

Lark Hill Camp was a soldier's city. Canteens and privately owned shops displayed a wonderful variety of goods, and restaurants presented appetising bills of fare.

Stonehenge, the haunt of the ancient Druids, was close at hand, and an interesting feature of the training grounds was this old-time place of strange worship, where the massive cromlechs stood grimly silent; and the tumuli, huge elongated mounds, or graves, dotted the country for miles around, and provided excellent cover for practise field operations.

Scarcely had the Battalion settled down to the new life in England when four days' disembarkation leave was granted. London attracted the majority, and the time spent in the great city was thoroughly enjoyed. Westminster Abbey, St. Paul's Cathedral, Parliament Houses, the Tower, and many places of historical interest were visited.

On returning to camp the Unit settled down to three months of solid training. Leave from camp was granted on Saturday and Sunday afternoons when delightful walks were taken through quaint villages, shady avenues of oaks and elms and on beds of bracken in the deeper shade of the woods men relaxed after a hard week's work and listened to the songs of the thrush.

After the Battalion had been vigorously training for about five weeks, H.M. the King desired to inspect the whole of the Third Division.

The review took place at Bulford Field, three miles distant from Lark Hill, where this Unit met the other Battalions of the Division and details of A.I.F. Units from various camps in the neighborhood and a detachment of New Zealand troops. The weather was inclined to be chilly, and while awaiting the arrival of His Majesty the men were invited to join in games and athletic contests.

When King George rode into Bulford Field the Division had been formed up in Battalions in line. Massed bands played the Royal Salute, and, as the Division presented arms thousands of bayonets flashed in the air, a long line of steel which stretched across the field until the bayonets in the distance looked like fine needles. When the Division had been inspected the Battalions marched past His Majesty in column of companies to the stirring strains of the massed bands.

Lieut.-Colonel C. H. Davis, of this Unit, with other Battalion commanders was afterwards presented to the King.

Everyone was in high spirits, and when at last His Majesty took his departure hats were placed on bayonets, and he was loudly cheered. In the month of October the Battalion had its first experience of trench life.

Leaving Lark Hill in daylight the Tenth Brigade (37th, 38th, 39th, 40th Battalions) marched to the Bustard Trenches, six miles out of camp, and experienced the unpleasant conditions of winter warfare. Rain swept the open country and poured into the white-chalk trenches. When at night several companies entered the trenches to take up their positions, men floundered through pools of whitewash, and got covered with sticky white mud. Verey lights went hissing up through the driving rain, to illuminate a dreary landscape. Rifles cracked, and the dull detonations of hand grenades momentarily drowned the angry hissing of the rain. Here and there feeble attempts had been made to build dug-outs, but these excavations were small, and afforded but poor protection from the weather. Men huddled up in their sodden overcoats and settled down to the long, dreary hours of darkness.

When morning broke, cold and cheerless, a hot breakfast arrived, and unhappy looking faces brightened considerably.

The Companies were relieved shortly afterwards and retired to billets where the miseries of the night were soon forgotten in sleep. The next three days were finer, although cold showers occasionally made things unpleasant; and everyone was glad when the time came to return to camp.

* * * *

CHAPTER II.—FRANCE.

In November, 1916, the Division was considered fit for service in France, and embarkation was commenced, this Unit embarking at Southampton on the afternoon of November 22. The embarkation of a fully-equipped Battalion is no small undertaking; horses, waggons, general supplies, and a thousand odds and ends have to be dealt with. Great satisfaction was, therefore, expressed by all concerned at this gigantic task being accomplished without a hitch.

The Channel was crossed during the hours of darkness, and the old French port of Le Havre was reached in the early hours of the morning, the Unit landing shortly after daylight.

After five months' absence from Australia the Thirty-eighth Battalion set foot upon the soil of France, where for two long years it was to face the bitter hardships of war.

The march through Le Havre proved interesting. Hundreds of women and children besieged the long khaki column, and did a brisk trade in fruit, chocolate and various confections.

The first attempt to "parley" with the French folk was truly amusing. But the novelty of the surroundings soon wore off as the weight of each man's gear began to tell upon his buoyant spirits.

This march to No. 2 Rest Camp was one of the hardest the Battalion ever had in France, although the distance was not great. The abnormal burden of pack, rifle, ammunition, blankets, etc., tested one's strength to the utmost, and a long, tortuous, uphill road which led to the camp seemed to add a hundred pounds weight to the already overburdened men, who were thoroughly exhausted on reaching the summit.

After a good dinner and afternoon's rest spirits revived, and next morning everybody looked fit for the march to the railway, where the Battalion was to entrain for the Front. This march proved much easier, for it was mostly downhill going.

At the railway everybody was busily employed loading the troop train, and it was growing dark ere the long line of carriages and trucks pulled out of Le Havre en route to Bailleul.

The journey proved a very tedious one.

For forty hours the train crawled along like a snail. The weather was cold, and to warm themselves the men often walked beside the train.

A story is related of one man, who, on alighting from the crawling train, said that he was going to gather some wayside flowers to send home to Australia. "But you won't find any flowers at this time of the year," said a comrade. "That's alright. I've got a packet of seed in my pocket," came the reply.

At Abbeville the train halted for a rest and went to sleep. About fifty of its passengers got out and went for a walk in search of hot coffee. But during their absence the train woke up and decided to shuffle along for a few more miles; and so they were left behind to await the next train going somewhere in the direction of the front.

Bailleul was reached at three o'clock on the morning of the 26th, when tired, cramped men awakened from fitful slumber to hear for the first time the dull booming of the guns of the Western Front, and see strange, fantastic lights illuminating the sky in the north.

To hear the guns of battle for the first time is a never-to-be-forgotten experience; a strange feeling not of fear or nervousness, but a sensation that is almost indefinable takes possession of one.

Perhaps there is a certain amount of mental excitement. One suddenly becomes curiously interested in those dull detonations and strange lights, and for a while does some very deep thinking.

It was a cheerless dawn which broke over the town of Bailleul. Men unloading the train were wet to the skin by driving showers of icy rain, and the raw air stung one's face and hands.

Fortunately, the rain ceased at daylight when motor buses conveyed the Battalion to Strezaele, about three miles distant.

Here the Unit was billeted in farm buildings which were scattered about the featureless country. Old ramshackle barns proved havens of rest to the worn-out men who stretched out on beds of clean straw, much to the disgust of the farm animals which were turned out of their winter quarters to make room for the intruders.

Two days were pleasantly passed at the old farm houses before moving on to Armentieres. The French folk made everyone thoroughly at home, and merry hours were spent before the blazing fires of farmhouse kitchens, drinking steaming coffee, sampling wines and struggling to learn the language of the country, much to the amusement of the farming people.

The first aerial battle witnessed by the Battalion took place at Strezaele, when two enemy scout 'planes were intercepted by a pair of Allied aeroplanes.

For ten minutes the machines circled, dived and ducked, and the rattle of their machine-guns was clearly heard. Finally the Boche finding the game too hot made off in the direction of the Front and managed to make their escape.

On the morning of the 28th November the Unit left Strezaele and marched to Armentieres, a distance of about twenty kilometres. Enemy aircraft interrupted the march for a short while when a friendly hedge screened the long column from the scout 'planes on the look-out for artillery targets.

On nearing Armentieres barbed wire entanglements were seen for the first time. When about to enter the town a warning was received that the Pont de Niappe causeway, which must be crossed, was under enemy observation and shell fire. Orders were given to don steel helmets, and the causeway was crossed by companies at two minute intervals. The thought of being under shell fire for the first time produced a mild feeling of excitement; but the crossing proved quite a tame affair, and it was not until six months afterwards that the causeway was shelled. It was growing dusk when the town was entered. The march had proved a tiring affair and everyone felt worn out. Armentieres on first acquaintance did not look a cheerful place, for the simple reason that the Battalion was introduced to it after nightfall, when all lights in the houses and cafes were obscured by heavy shutters on account of enemy bombing 'planes. At that time one little dreamed that behind those shutters was many a gay and homely scene, and that some of the happiest times ever to be spent in France awaited the Battalion in the old town of Armentieres.

A large factory in Barbed-Wire Square accommodated the tired travellers, and here the next three days were spent in preparation for the first trip into the trenches.

Equipment kits and gas masks were carefully inspected, and every care taken that the men were provided with everything necessary for their personal comfort and welfare. It is seldom that one unit relieves another in broad daylight, but at Armentieres reliefs were often carried out in the daytime, for the communication trenches which led to the defences on the outskirts of the town were screened by buildings, and could not be observed by the enemy.

At 8 a.m. on December 1st the Battalion left billets to relieve New Zealand troops in the left sub-sector, Houplines area, and proceeded by half platoons to Little Mary Dump, and was issued with gum-boots which were put on before entering the communication trenches. These trenches were very deep and narrow. Duckboards bridging the mud were broken in places, and the result was that men often found themselves waist deep in slimy mud, or sprawling full length into icy cold slush. Irish Avenue was in a particularly vile condition, and the officers and men of "C" and "D" Companies struggled along this narrow, slimy passage through water up to their waists.

The subsidiary, support, and front-line trenches were reached after an hour's hard struggle through muddy walls where men got jammed, soaked through to the skin with icy water, and plastered with mud. The day was fairly quiet; odd shells occasionally livened things up, and these explosions were curiously watched. Dugouts afforded but a minimum amount of shelter from the inclement weather, for water dripped through their rusty iron roofs, and oozed through the mud walls. High breastworks screened all movements from the enemy, and over these solidly-built banks the men in the front line peered for the first time into No Man's Land. These breastworks were subjected to Minenwerfer bombardments and had to be constantly repaired. The distance across No Man's Land varied from 80 to 200 yards. On the left of the sub-sector, and just within the enemy territory, was the shattered village of Frelingham. Whenever a breach was made in the breastworks snipers hidden in the ruins of Frelingham made things very lively for those who repaired the damaged bank.

A hundred yards in rear of the front line a dummy support trench attracted considerable fire from the enemy, and was daily battered by heavy trench mortars. The area between the subsidiary and front line trenches were pitted with deep "Minnie" holes filled with muddy water. Living conditions were appalling. Hands gathered mud from everything that was touched. For ten days the Battalion held the sub-sector and wallowed in mud day and night. It was really a quiet time, for weather conditions prevented much being done in the way of warfare.

Two hot meals were served every day, and hot cocoa at midnight. To guard against trench feet, socks were changed daily, and feet well rubbed with whale oil.

Captain G. V. Lansell, a most capable and popular officer, was wounded on 3rd December, 1916, and his wounds proving serious and causing him to relinquish the game of war he was invalided back to Australia.

Taking advantage of a favorable wind, gas was released against the enemy trenches on December 4th, and drifted across No Man's Land in fleecy clouds. The enemy's gas alarms sounded for miles along his lines, but no results were afterwards visable.

On the night of the 10th December the observers on Lewis Gun posts in the trench occupied by "B" Company became suspicious that the barbed wire entanglements which protected the trench were being cut. An occasional click could be heard in No Man's Land, and presently a shadowy form was observed moving cautiously about in the dark.

A Verey light was sent up to illuminate the neighborhood under suspicion, and revealed a Boche rapidly seeking cover in a shell hole. Shots were fired at him, and immediately enemy trench mortars made things lively for "B" Company's men. The shells crashed about the trench for three very long minutes. A Lewis Gun was put out of action and a bombing post was blown in.

Directly the shelling ceased about twelve Boche rushed the parapet and bombed the trench, but cool and determined men quickly drove them off with rifle fire into the blackness of No Man's Land. Second-Lieut. K. G. Emmonson, Trench Officer, and three other ranks were wounded whilst pluckily defending their position and routing the enemy.

The plucky Lieutenant was awarded the first Military Cross won in the Division, and Private J. J. Meyerink was awarded the Military Medal for bravely mounting the parapet and struggling to work a damaged machine gun.

The Unit was relieved by the Fortieth Battalion on the evening of the 10th December, and retired to billets in Armentieres.

After the miseries of the trenches, what palaces were the warm, brightly-lit cafes. Here was laughter, gaiety and the sparkle of bright eyes, and as charming Mimi served glasses of coffee, and blue spirals of cigarette smoke floated up to the ceiling, the mud and discomforts of the past ten days were completely forgotten.

It was hard to realise that Armentieres was so close to the firing line, and that at any moment enemy guns could pour salvo after salvo of screaming shells into the shops and factories where the civilians calmly went about their business, and seemed to be quite indifferent to any danger. And out in the fields farming operations were carried on even to within a mile of the line. Shells might drone overhead, but M. le Fermier and his horses continued to turn over the soil.

Half-past Eleven Square was a popular rendezvous, and here the events of the day or the latest news from Australia would be discussed. A neighboring tower had been hit by a shell, and the old clock which stared down into the square had stopped at eleven-thirty when the shell had smashed into the tower, and so the place had been given this strange name.

Civilians and soldiers rubbed shoulders in the Rue de Lille and Rue Sadi Carnot. Shop windows displayed attractive goods in the daytime, but at night business was carried on behind heavy shutters and closed doors.

A soldier's life in Armentieres was a strange mixture of events. It was not all rest and pleasure. Fatigue parties worked day and night shifts carrying ammunition, gas cylinders, etc., up to the trenches.

One night Private "Digger" would be floundering along in the mud, cursing the heavy gas cylinders, and listening to the sickening crunch of an exploding "Minnie" which seemed to shake the ground from under him.

On the following night he would be comfortably seated before a blazing fire with fair Marie correcting his French, and Grandmere nodding over her knitting. Could you have peeped in through the heavily-shuttered window you would have thought that he could not have looked more thoroughly at home had he been sitting at his own fireside in far-away Australia.

Armentieres has well been called the "Nursery of the Third Division." Walk into almost any French home at night and there you would find an Australian soldier.

Firm friendships were formed with the large-hearted townpeople, and many men of the Third Division will often look back with pleasure to the days of Armentieres.

On the 16th of December the Battalion again went into the trenches, spent five more days in the mud and rain, and then retired to billets in Houplines.

On Christmas Eve, under cover of darkness, men groped their way about in the open spaces in search of greenery to decorate their billets.

Next morning the rooms of many a shell-shocked house were brightly decorated with greenery, and Christmas greetings were chalked on the walls. Happy little companies sat down at midday to roast beef and plum pudding, and for awhile forgot all about the war. Lieut.-General Godley, Corps Commander, paid the Battalion a visit, and in a bright little speech said he hoped that the next Christmas dinner would be eaten in Australia.

But two more Christmas Days were yet to be spent in France.

At one o'clock on New Year's morning simultaneous raids were made along the whole Divisional front. The 38th Battalion had four raiding parties out, none of which, owing to uncut wire and detection by the Boche, effected an entry. The parties consisting of from 12 to 18 men apiece were commanded respectively by Lieut. Peters and Second-Lieutenant Spark on the right, and Second-Lieutenant Herring and Second-Lieutenant Pooley on the left. The latter party's attempt was made opposite a notorious point in the enemy trenches known as Raid Ditch. While the leading men were cutting the wire the party was caught in the bright beam of one of the enemy's searchlights constantly in use on this front. A withering fire from rifles and machine guns was immediately concentrated on the unlucky party—which, owing to the intensity of the fire was compelled to take whatever cover was available. In addition, the Boche freely hurled bombs and hand grenades into their midst. Heavy casualties resulted at once, those killed including Second-Lieut. Pooley. Sgt. W. L. Rowe (now Lieut.) thereupon took charge, with Corporal H. F. Poole (now Lieut.) as second in command. On the fire slackening somewhat they ascertained those who were alive, and later on led the survivors back to our lines.

Even the cover provided by the surrounding shell holes was insufficient to protect the few survivors from being hit, and the slightest raising of the body spelt death.

The Germans kept up their continuous fire for about half an hour, the whole of which time Sergeant Rowe and his comrades suffered an ordeal few others have experienced.

It was not until nearly 4 a.m. that the watchers in our trenches, by now almost devoid of hope, saw several figures silhouetted on our parapet, and one by one Sgt. Rowe and four others dropped into our trenches, utterly worn out and exhausted after their terrible experience. They were met by Major Hurry, who throughout the long hours had maintained a constant vigil. At daylight one more survivor, Pte. Lockett, returned—a total of six out of the eighteen who went over.

For this and other fine work Sgt. Rowe and Cpl. Poole were shortly afterwards promoted to commissioned rank.

On the following night Lieut. Peters led a relief party into No Man's Land to look for the missing men. Despite the searchlights and machine gun fire, a methodical search was made, and he and L.-Cpl. F. J. Perry (who was later in the year awarded the D.C.M. for conspicuous work as a Scout) located and brought back one of the ill-fated party who had been wounded, and though in a state of exhaustion through exposure was crawling towards our trenches.

For this and his good work on the previous night Lieut. Peters was awarded the M.C.

On the 13th January the whole front was heavily bombarded by the enemy. Minnenwerfer, high explosive and shrapnel being freely used.

Great damage was done to the trenches. Cambridge Avenue —a communication trench—was badly battered. The Battalion suffered several casualties, four other ranks being killed and seven put out of action through wounds and shell-shock. On the following day the Unit once again returned to billets, but not for a time of rest. Irish Avenue was in such a fearful condition owing to the weather that it was decided to dig another communication trench leading through to the front line. This work was done at night-time by a large working party of two hundred men who experienced some very lively times. Enemy searchlights occasionally swept the area, and showed up the large body of men struggling to dig down into the sticky ground and thus secure shelter from the machine gun bullets which whizzed through the night, and "plopped" into the mud. On the night of the 16th January 2nd-Lieut. Thompson (who had just received his commission) and Corporal Henry were killed by machine gun fire, and several men were wounded.

Those early days, while the Division was still untried; when all were as soldiers very young, none could deny everyone's keenness and eagerness to "get on with the war," and to "kill the Boche." "The Raiding Days" were as school days, the minor operation, a school for the "Magnus Opus," for a raid carried out with thoroughness was, indeed, the miniature of a battle.

Raiding trained officers in the marvellous amount of correct detail necessary in a fighting force; trained them, too, in leadership; taught everyone to regard an artillery barrage as a good friend, and how near that friend one could move unharmed; taught all to adhere to organisation and plans in the most trying circumstances, and, most of all, it revealed the Australian's superiority over the Boche.

But the raids served military purposes other than as schools —for clean steel was dipped in enemy blood. The raiders' activities fatigued and demoralised the enemy, and after every raid they knew his strength was minus many casualties, and his morale lower. Knew, too, that these raiding activities tied down on the northern front regiments of the enemy which would otherwise have gone south, to be thrown against Australian Divisions then fighting against great odds on the terrible Somme battlefields. Yes, the lads of "The Eggs-a-Cook" thought often of the older sister divisions and wished to be with them, but that not being possible helped all they could, and that by raiding. Less than three weeks after first entering the trenches "raids" were whispered of: then choice parties of men and a few officers passed from the Battalion and entered upon special training at the shell-torn Ecole Professionale in Armentieres. Efforts were made at secrecy, but all camouflage failed and added only an air of romance to the enterprises.

It may not be said that crowds rushed to volunteer for the raids, but always there were sufficient volunteers, and always men disappointed at being overlooked or omitted when any raiding party was made up.

But it can be said that always the choicest, cheeriest spirits, always the pick, found their way into the raiding parties.

What called them? Why was it that these men would at all times be willing to exchange the comparative safety of trench defence to take the unequal risk of a small party of bold men, matched against seemingly every German, every machine gun, every minenwerfer, rifle and field gun adjacent to the raided locality? Was it that they wished to gain in warlike experience, or hungered for war trophies; or, perhaps, desired to appear (as they did) amongst their comrades as super-soldiers? It might have been any of these, but it is doubtful.

Rather, one thinks, 'twas the old lure of Romance, that twain Mystery and Adventure, which lured our pioneers, hardiest sons of a hardy nation, to our own Southern Land, that now sent their descendants "over the top" raiding. Mystery, born of the night, when the perilous reconnaissance of No Man's Land was made, and the scouts stealthily crawling along the enemy entanglements heard the movements of the foe, the handling of arms, footsteps on duckboards, his speech and even his songs as some incautious sentry cheered his lonely vigil.

And Mystery of Mysteries when, on the night before the raid, the enemy entanglements smashed by trench mortars had to be examined, and a gap proved before the raid could be launched; when with caution, mud and slime from head to foot, the scouts, silent as shadows and almost as elusive, elbowed, crawled and sidled their way through "the gap," and close to the enemy parapet.

On the 28th January a raiding party drawn from all Units of the Tenth Brigade gave the Boche a lively time, bombing his dugouts and killing and wounding a number of men.

The first prisoner captured by the Third Division was brought in by the elated men of the Thirty-ninth Battalion.

Next morning two companies of the 38th Battalion and two of the 37th Battalion forming a unit of 800 strong, under Lieut.-Col. Davis, retired to billets at Erquinghem Baths, for special training as a raiding Battalion. The remainder of the two Battalions, under Major R. O. Henderson, was known as X Battalion. This unit was in and out of the trenches in Bois Grenier sector while the raiders were training at Erquinghem, and it experienced some very rough times. Two officers, 2nd-Lieut. Thomas and 2nd-Lieut. Watson were killed in action on 1st and 23rd February respectively.

The days with the raiding battalion were busy ones. The weather was bitterly cold, but the work of training kept the blood freely circulating, and this meant warm bodies. Flooded fields had frozen, and many hours were spent skating on the slippery ice. Everyone was new at the game, casualties occurred; heads, arms and legs being broken, until at last orders prohibited this enjoyable but risky sport.

From an aerial photograph of enemy trenches to be raided a trench system was marked out so that everyone should be familiar with it. But when it came to digging the frozen ground picks and shovels burred, and after several days of hard work the trenches were only six inches deep, and the job was given up as a hopeless one.

These days of training were enjoyed by all, despite the bitterness of the weather. France was experiencing the coldest winter of thirty years; rivers and canals were frozen feet deep.

Wash a handkerchief in boiling water, then wave it in the air for a few seconds, and, lo and behold! your fingers grasped a stiff, frozen piece of linen. Men usually drank their tea directly it was served, for if left in a mess tin for a few minutes it would bcome a lump of brown ice.

On one occasion two men decided to have some jelly with their evening meal. A packet of jelly crystals had arrived in a parcel sent from Australia. So boiling water was procured, and a mess tin full of pink jelly was quickly made. Tea not yet being ready, the mess tin was put aside. Later on, when the two friends sat down to enjoy their jelly they found that it had frozen. The hard pink lump was knocked out of the tin, and cracked up into pieces with an entrenching tool.

No intelligence regarding the date of the raid was forthcoming. On the night of the 24th (known as W night) the Raiding Battalion marched out from billets to all appearances bound for the trenches, but after being away for two hours returned to Erquinghem. This trip was made to deceive spies in the neighborhood who were, no doubt, keeping a sharp eye on the movements of the raiders, and had means of communication with the enemy. A heavy barrage was put down on the enemy trenches, and, from information afterwards received the Boche expected it would be followed by an infantry attack.

However, when the barrage ceased he was left in peace to ponder over matters.

On X night, the 25th, the Battalion again left billets, and again returned without paying a visit to the front line. Another barrage swept the enemy trenches.

On Y night the raiders kept to their billets, and the enemy was not disturbed by the artillery. But on Z night the 27th January, the raiders left billets and marched about two and a half miles out of Erquinghem and were picked up by motor lorries and conveyed to Armentieres, where they disappeared into the communication trenches.

At 10 p.m., while the Raiders were proceeding from the motor lorries to the trenches, a preliminary short, but intense, artillery shoot took place. This diversion lasted for 20 minutes, the area to be raided at 12.30 being heavily bombarded by our 18 pounders and 4.5in Hows. This undoubtedly enabled the Raiders to effect a surprise at 2.30 a.m.

The comparative quietness of our guns between 10.20 and zero hour apparently convinced the Boche he had received his "full issue" for that night.

At midnight six hundred and fifty raiders, with blackened faces, noiselessly left the safe cover of the friendly trenches, crawled out over the parapet, through our own scanty wire to lay up cold and still and silent, awaiting zero hour. While lying there unseen, bullets from enemy machine guns crashed and whistled above them; rockets soared and burst in dazzling radiance, and beams from enemy searchlights swept No Man's Land.

Twelve-thirty, which was zero hour, brought on hurricane wings the barrage when our batteries with splendid synchronization and marvellous accuracy sent a tornado of high explosive and shrapnel on the enemy front line, killing, wounding and demoralising the enemy watchers; while those in dugouts were prevented from leaving them.

All this while the raiders rapidly approached their objective. Never will that moment be forgotten. No Man's Land lit by the panic rockets of the enemy, red, white, green and yellow, and luminous with the flash of bursting shell; ears filled with the smash and crash of the barrage, and nostrils with the intoxicating smell of burnt powder. There, spread over a front of half a mile, were running figures, the raiders, six hundred and fifty of them, showing black in the glare as they ran toward the German trenches, some with little weight, and some burdened with mats and bridges to overcome enemy obstacles and charges to demolish dugouts: everyone and everything according to plan. The first check was "The Willow Ditch." The scouts had measured it, and here a light bridge was rushed into place and almost no seconds were lost. The raiders streamed through the gaps, past wire torn apart and thrown back in confused masses by trench mortar bombs, and paused for a short spell forty yards from the enemy parapet.

Bursting lungs gasped for breath until the barrage lifted from the front line.

Then the raiders moved on.

Close to the parapet Fritz had restored one belt of wire. A powerful raider swung a straw mat on to it; on that he jumped, swung another mat forward, and so on. Meanwhile, on each side of him, men with huge wire-cutters hacked at the wire until it fell, leaving a straw-matted path over which the raiders

I.—STRAZEELE: THE BATTALION'S FIRST BILLETS IN FRANCE.

II.—HALF-PAST ELEVEN SQUARE, ARMENTIERES.

III.—THROUGH ARMENTIERES TO THE FRONT LINE.

LEADING.—L.CPL. J. C. LEWIS. L.CPL. NEWELL. SGT. PANKHURST. PTE. LOADER

ran. Then came the enemy borrow ditch, 8ft wide, 5ft deep and filled with loose wire and water—a difficult obstacle, but a bridge had been made for crossing it. But the bridge was not there. Its carriers had become casualties and it lay in shell-torn fragments.

It did not matter, for the raiders chanced on the enemy's sally-post, a banked-up track through the ditch, crossed it, rushed on to the parapet and looked down into the enemy trench. A Fritz is leaving a dug-out just below them; he sees them; jumps back and endeavors to close the small iron door. No use, a shot from a revolver and the door swings open. But Fitz has gone downstairs. He does not come up, although the raiders with German phrases tell him "It is alright," so the pin is drawn from a Mill's bomb, which is thrown down the dugout.

A shriek as one Boche dies, then six others cry "Kamarad," come up, and are sent to the lines as prisoners.

The raiders streamed on. Successive parties attacked the second and third line as the barrage moved back; then, while the area, 800 yards wide and 350 yards deep, was being cleaned up, the barrage settled down in a protection "box" clear of the flanks and rear, protecting parties from a counter-attack.

A captured machine gun, a searchlight (the first ever captured) and a few prisoners come from the trenches.

A loud roar as one party explodes a dump of minenwerfer, and smaller detonations where doors and dugouts are blown in, often entombing those inside; Boche who refused an invitation to "Come out." Many surrendered; a few put up a plucky fight, but quickly learned the quality of the Australian bayonet.

Enemy material everywhere was destroyed, fires were started here and there, the raiders revelling in an orgy of destruction, determined that this sector should be so utterly wrecked that many months would pass before it could be re-organised and re-equipped. Hundreds of bombs, scores of rifles and dozens of snipers plates, too heavy to carry away, were hurled over the parapets and splashed into the water-logged borrow-ditch, lost forever to the German army.

Meanwhile, the barrage continued in its protective fire, forming a "box" at the rear and flanks. 'Twas a sight for admiration and ever to be remembered. Our gunners demonstrated their marvellous efficiency, and the raiders were loud in their praise. "Why!" said one, "the barrage line was so straight that you could have toasted bread at it." Truly a risky experiment, but, nevertheless, high praise.

One small counter attack was made. 'Twas half-hearted, however, and entirely lost heart and broke when it met a third line party of raiders which engaged it with Lewis Gun, rifle, bayonet and revolver.

The raiders had been in the enemy trenches for thirty-five minutes when the time for the withdrawal arrived, and the word "Out" was passed. Systematically the raiders moved back, first the third line parties; then the second line; then the scouts and matmen, each covering the others movements.

Satisfied that all had reported to him the O.C. Assault cut the telephone wire, the signallers picked up the 'phone and completed the stream of men moving toward their own line.

A raider was heard singing, "And we really had a most delightful evening." And so they had, but what about Fritz?

The enemy's resistance had been at first by machine gun fire from concrete emplacements ,and he had caused casualties during the raiders' progress across No Man's Land. A storming party had been wiped out by a chance "pineapple" when moving out from the trench, necessitating a re-organisation at almost the last minute.

At zero. plus two minutes, the enemy had placed down his S.O.S., or protective barrage, which claimed its toll in killed and wounded; but neither that nor any other of his defences prevented the raiders entering his trenches.

Out of all the 38th men engaged, casualties amounted to only sixteen killed and forty-five wounded. Besides the seventeen prisoners sent back, it is estimated conservatively that over two hundred enemy dead were left about when the raiders withdrew. So one of the objectives showed the credit balance on the side of the raiders—Twelve (12) Boche dead for one Australian.

Once the raiders were within their own territory they moved rapidly by overland tracks and through communication trenches to the checking station, where they handed over their identity labels and spoil, and received a fine ration of rum; then, mounting the motor lorries waiting in the streets of Houplines they were conveyed to their billets at Erquinghem, where they told their stories, exhibited their souvenirs and fought the raid over again before turning in for their well-earned rest; while wearily the officers labored over their reports until well after daylight.

All the usual raiding objectives were achieved.

The capture and destruction of enemy personnel, equipment, defence material and arms was complete and huge. The important items to the Intelligence Service were specimens of a Minenwerfer fuse, and the first searchlight ever captured, which showed improvements unknown to our own manufacturers.

Lieutenant-Colonel C. H. Davis, of the 38th Battalion (Commanding the Raiding Battalion) who had skilfully planned the raid, had again proved himself a most capable leader, and it was in recognition of much splendid work such as the big raid at Houplines, that he was a few months later awarded the Distinguished Service Order.

Company Commanders were:—"A" Company (37th Batt.), Capt. W. F. H. Robertson. "B" Company (38th Batt.), Capt. J. Akeroyd. "C" Company (38th Batt.), Capt. F. E. Fairweather. "D" Company (37th Batt.), Capt. W. J. Symons, V.C.

Capt. J. A. Akeroyd, who was among the wounded, was rendered unfit for further service in France, and returned to Australia at a later date.

The day after the raid, X Battalion joined the raiders at Erquinghem Baths, when the 37th and 38th Battalions were reformed. The latter unit relieved the 40th Battalion in the left sub-sector of Bois Gremier on 2nd March, and was relieved by the 4th South Lancashires eight days later, when it again retired to Erquinghem, and billeted for the night en route to Steinwerck for a short period of special practise in the initial training of a new formation of attack.

Ten days were spent at Steinwerck, and on the Third Division retiring for a few weeks' rest from warfare, the Battalion marched back to Morninghem in easy stages, via Hazebrouck and Wardrecques.

The fortnight spent at Moringhem was not a pleasant time. The weather was bitterly cold and stormy. Deep snow covered the ground, and driving showers of rain constantly swept the countryside. On one occasion when the Battalion was returning to billets from a Brigade practise in attack, it was caught in a blizzard. Clouds of hard, fine snow beat down upon the column, stinging and blinding everyone. With bowed heads, and faces covered with aching hands, the Battalion struggled on through snowdrifts, and half smothered by the choking particles, finally reached billets.

On April 5th the Unit started back for the line, and experienced one of the worst marches it ever had. Deep snow checked the footsteps of the men struggling along with heavy packs and equipment. Lewis gunners dragged small handcarts loaded with guns and ammunition. The wheels of these carts often sank down into soft beds of snow, when the gunners had a bad time of it. By devious routes which unnecessarily extended the march, the Battalion, worn out and fit to drop, reached Wallan Capelle at dusk, where it was billeted for the night. The arrival of the motor lorries bringing the blankets was eagerly awaited.

But it was not until one o'clock in the morning that they turned up; so, for about six hours, worn-out men shivered with the coldness of the night.

The march was resumed next morning. Weather conditions had slightly improved, but the day's journey of twenty-two miles was a severe test, and when after eight p.m. the Battalion entered Armentieres feet were blistered, and men hobbled painfully along the hard cobblestone roads.

It is truly wonderful how quickly men will recover from an exhausting march. Next morning, apart from sore feet and a certain amount of stiffness, everyone looked fit. The march was discussed in rather ornate language; but now it was one of many bitter experiences which belonged to the past, and one could afford to joke about unpleasant incidents of the past two days.

Armentieres residents gave the Unit a hearty welcome back to the old town, and the next ten days were very pleasant ones. The Y.M.C.A. cinema, and the "Coo-ees" 3rd Divisional Concert Party, attracted large audiences with their splendid programmes.

On the 16th April the left sector at Houplines was taken over from the 40th Battalion. Here the trenches were in good condition, and strongly-built dugouts roofed with bow iron proved weatherproof and comfortable. Artillery daily strafed the enemy who always retaliated. While these artillery duels were fought the front line was practically vacated, for the enemy always battered the breastworks.

The Battalion was relieved on the 26th April by the 2/6 King's Own Liverpool Regiment and three days later retired to Oosthove Farm, in Ploegsteert-St. Yves sector, as a reserve battalion.

Here a very enjoyable fortnight was spent. Comfortable huts and a large farmhouse which was surrounded by a moat, accommodated the Unit. The days were warm with early Spring sunshine; budding trees rapidly unfolded bright green leaves; and in the fields buttercups and daisies peeped up through the young grass. In the daytime working parties dug gun pits and cable trenches a few miles out from the farm. This work was done under pleasant conditions, and proved enjoyable exercise.

Towards the end of the stay the quietness of Oosthove Farm was rudely disturbed for two nights. Short intense shoots by the artillery on the whole of the Corps front awakened the enemy guns, and a neighboring battery drew shell-fire upon the farm when everyone sought shelter in the surrounding fields and slept out in the open.

On the 13th May the Unit moved up into Ploegsteert Wood to relieve the 40th Battalion at Rifle House, and be in support to the 37th Battalion. Entering the wood was like passing into Fairyland. Here Spring reigned in all her fresh, sweet beauty. Golden shafts of sunshine pierced leafy canopies, and quivered in beds of bright green grasses. Pale yellow primroses, golden buttercups, and white daisies embroidered the green carpet of the wood, which stole all noises from the foot. Clusters of dark violets peeped out from mossy beds, and seas of pale blue hyacinths bent their heads to the breezes. Duckboard tracks wound in and out among flaming copper beeches and pink blossomed chestnuts.

Before war broke out Ploegsteert Wood was the hunting ground of the King of Belgium. Beautiful as it now was what must its peaceful beauty have been in those days. Now the harsh barking of eighteen-pounders interrupted the song birds as they flooded the sunny glades with melody. The duckboard tracks running through the wood were named after London streets. Picadilly Circus, The Strand, Regent Street, Haymarket and many other familiar names greeted one from fingerposts. Rifle House, where Battalion Headquarters was established, was in the neighborhood of Picadilly Circus. This building, like most of the homes in the wood, had sandbag walls, and was roofed with old iron. Perhaps the finest building in the wood was Ploegsteert Hall, which was at one time Captain Bruce Bairnsfather's Company Headquarters. It was built of logs in the Canadian style, and here the famous artist drew many of his well-known pictures. Ploegsteert Hall was afterwards destroyed by shell-fire and its original sign was salved from the ruins by Lieut.-Colonel (then Major) Hurry of this Battalion, who presented it to the A.I.F. War Records Section.

Life in the woods for the next few days was delightful. Men stretched themselves out on grassy beds and enjoyed the warm sunshine.

Enemy aeroplanes would sometimes pass overhead, but the leafy trees screened all movements in the wood. All day long the eighteen pounders roared among the trees, and shells screamed over to the enemy.

Fresh batteries took up their positions and it was not long before enemy shells were searching for them. From this time onward the Battalion was subjected to a good deal of shell-fire. One night the enemy guns poured salvo after salvo into the neighborhood of Rifle House, and for an hour the air was full of flying wood and iron.

To the enemy there must have been every indication of a coming offensive, for the increase of guns which continually harassed him for miles along the line spoke of a big battle in the near future.

On the 22nd May the Battalion moved forward and relieved the 37th Battalion in the front line beyond the wood. Next day another Unit took over a portion of the front, the 38th Battalion holding from Ainscroft Avenue to Ash Lane.

A raiding party of seven officers and 214 other ranks chosen from all companies attacked the enemy at two o'clock on the morning of the 28th. The party was divided into two columns of which one effected an entry into the enemy's trench and brought back a prisoner. Unfortunately the raiding party suffered heavy casualties, many of which were caused by our own barrage. Two officers (2nd-Lieuts. Killingsworth and Blair) and twenty-eight other ranks were killed or missing; two officers and sixty-three other ranks being wounded.

Lieuts. W. H. McCullock and T. H. Kennedy were awarded the Military Cross for courageous conduct in the face of the enemy. Lieut. Kennedy, although wounded in his right hand, attacked a party of the enemy, killing several, and forcing a sergeant-major to surrender at the point of an empty pistol grasped in his wounded hand. Pte. F. Lock was awarded the D.C.M. for conspicuous bravery.

CHAPTER III.

BATTLES OF MESSINES, YPRES AND PASSCHENDAELE.

On the 2nd of June the Battalion was relieved and retired to Brune Gay to prepare for the great battle of Messines of June 7th.

Previous to the Battalion moving out from the wood Lieut. Hyett, who had just been appointed Burial Officer to the Third Division, paid his old friends a visit, and on his way back to Division was killed by a shell at Hyde Park Corner.

At Brune Gay several interesting days were spent studying a model of the area to be attacked by the Third Division. This model was a wonderful piece of work; miniature hills, woods, winding rivers, and the battered town of Messines had been cleverly and artistically made, and one looked down upon them as an airman might study country lying a thousand feet below. Lectures were given, and important features of the country were pointed out so that everyone should be quite familiar with them.

Kits and equipment were overhauled and every preparation for the attack was made.

The day on which it was to be launched upon the enemy was not disclosed until six p.m. on June 6th when everyone was warned to be in readiness to move up to the "jumping off" positions in four hours time. Bombs, picks, shovels, and forty-eight hours rations were issued; and after being served with a hot meal, at 9.30 the Battalion moved forward by platoons.

The march up to the line was a fearful ordeal. Ten minutes after leaving Brune Gay the enemy bombarded the roads with gas shells. The night was sultry, and gas masks almost suffocated everyone; while the mica eyepieces became blurred, making it difficult for men to keep in touch with one another. Added to this the roads were badly congested with traffic; ammunition columns often blocked the way, and, here and there shattered waggons and horses were strewn across the roads. At last it became utterly impossible to make any headway, so the Battalion took to the open fields and groped its way through Ploegsteert Wood.

But the Wood also proved a hot corner. Shells were crashing in among the trees, and whirlwinds of wood and iron swept down upon the half suffocated men, who, through the dimmed windows of their masks sought to penetrate the inky blackness of the Wood.

Every now and then men lost touch with their comrades and wandered away from the duckboard tracks (which could only be seen when lit up by a bursting shell) to become lost among the trees. Others fell wounded by the way, and patiently waited for the stretcher-bearers.

At 2 a.m. the jumping off positions were reached by the exhausted and disorganised parties. These particular trenches had been specially dug for the attack and were situated about midway between the front and support lines, a rough, shallow, quickly-dug line, but, nevertheless, a haven of rest after that nightmare of an approach march. In places the line ran over high ground clear of the gas and those troops fortunate to be occupying these positions could remove their masks and drink in the fresh air.

Zero Hour was fixed for 3.10 a.m. and while awaiting that hour parties were rearranged for the attack. All were eager for the "hop off" and were keen on getting "some of their own" back on the enemy who had given them such a rough time for the past two hours or more. All felt positive of success on account of the elaborate preparations which had been made for

HISTORY OF 38th BATTALION, A.I.F.

the "stunt"; and, furthermore by the fact that every man knew exactly the nature of the job ahead of him, being in possession of almost as much information regarding the operation as the most senior officer.

Waiting to "hop off" creates a nervous tension. As the hands of the watch creep slowly, oh! how slowly, on toward zero hour a feeling of restlessness creeps along the line. Hands reach for the rifles lying against the side of the trench, and presently the bayonets commence to quiver. The limbs of strong, eager men quiver with an excitement which refuses to be calmed. Men constantly peer into the luminous faces of their watches.

Surely the blessed "ticker" has stopped!

A trembling hand puts the watch to an ear. An excited brain almost refuses to register the calm little "tick-tick, tick-tick." Yes, it is going alright, but, dear God! how slowly. An evil spirit seems to have put a brake on the wheels.

And so the minutes crawl slowly on, and men count every passing second, and in an attempt to check their excitement again review the movements which are to take place when those long minutes have dragged out their existence. The attack is to be made in three waves.

First Wave.—"D" Company (Major A. J. A. Maudsley, O.C.) with 5 and 6 Platoons of "B" Company.

Second Wave.—"A" Company (Captain R. E. Trebilcock, O.C.) with 7 and 8 Platoons of "B" Company.

Third Wave.—"C" Company (Captain F. E. Fairweather, O.C.).

The task allotted to the First Wave is that of capturing Ungodly Trench and establishing a line slightly in advance of it joining up with the New Zealanders on the left and the 39th Battalion on the right.

The Second Wave is to mop up in rear of the First and then continue the advance through Ungodly Trench to a distance of about 800 yards and there consolidate, this to be known as the Black Line. New Zealand troops to be on the left and the 9th Brigade on the right.

The Third Wave is to mop up for the Second and it also is to be consolidated in rear of the Black Line. One Company of the 40th Battalion is to build bridges across the La Douve River to allow the attackers to cross.

The barrage is to take the form of a "jumping barrage", 500 yards every three minutes, with the following exceptions:— To rest for a period of 37 minutes on Ulcer Reserve line; one hour seven minutes on Ungodly Trench, and a further period of six hours in front of the Black Line. The barrage would include machine gun fire with artillery, and from what one knew of its strength and staying powers there would not be many Boche left in those places to meet the attackers. The signal for the barrage to open out would be the exploding of the mines under the enemy trenches in the village of Messines. Engineers had tunnelled under the hill in a most wonderful way and had prepared a fearful death-trap for the enemy.

"Tick-tick, tick-tick," the little luminous hands are ticking out the remaining seconds. Men brace themselves for the attack, and then—the success of the great work the engineers and miners had been toiling at for months past was revealed to them.

First of all the ground shook under the attacking troops with earthquake effect. For one alarming moment it seemed that the earth would belly up and hurl them into eternity. And then the shaking underfoot abruptly ceased; and half-left. at Messines a volcano shot a volume of flame skyward sweeping aside the grey light of dawn, and flooding the countryside with blood-red light. A sickening, crunching roar shook the air, reverberated through the aisles of Ploegsteert Wood; and echoed along valleys and among hills for miles and miles around.

And so with one loud, fearful cry the tortured earth gave birth to death and destruction. And as that all-fearful voice died down the roar of the barrage challenged the enemy guns. Thousands of steel throats were belching forth flame and smoke, and hurling tons of screaming iron down upon the enemy. Machine gun bullets were forming a leaden curtain above the heads of the attackers, a curtain which spread out to the enemy. The effect of the exploding of the mines, and the confident roar of the barrage had an excellent moral effect upon the storming troops, a battle tonic which sent the First Wave clambering out of the trenches, while with difficulty the Second and Third Waves were restrained from joining them. The feeling of restlessness now took flight and with light hearts they pressed on to their objective. Although the ground passed over was extremely rough, being a wilderness of shell holes, the old front line of trenches was soon crossed. 'Twas not long ere the Second Wave had overtaken the First which had successfully gained its objective.

Aeroplanes had marked the positions of enemy batteries and had almost immediately silenced many of their voices as they opened out in reply. But there were still many guns active and shells burst about the attackers, the noise of their explosions being unheard on account of the terrific roar of our barrage. The only knowledge of the presence of an enemy shell was that the concussion would be felt or casualties would be observed.

The artillery barrage was so accurate that men quickly gained confidence to rest almost under the shrapnel bursts as they waited for them to lift farther back.

The Second Wave had now reached the river and to their great consternation discovered that the bridges for crossing had not been put into position. In one place a tree had fallen across the stream and this was used as a bridge by many of the troops. A number waded through the water in shallow places but experienced difficulty on account of wire. Ulcer Reserve was reached with a minimum of casualties. During the 37 minutes which elapsed while waiting for the barrage to lift all trenches were stormed and mopped up when many prisoners we e taken.

The barrage lifting again the attackers pressed on meeting very little opposition and finally arrived in rear of the fiery curtain licking up Ungodly Trench for one hour and seven minutes to enable the New Zealanders to come up on the left.

At this stage all three waves were together, and men quickly got busy on shell holes making themselves as safe as possible from enemy shell fire. Nothing of note happened during this rest. This barrage continued to lick up Ungodly Trench while the waves were re-organised for the continuance of the advance. Men were fatigued after the trying and exciting night and the dawn's work, and despite the deafening crashes of shells many fell asleep.

At last the barrage lifted. On went the First Wave, storming what was left of Ungodly Trench, and on to capture Schnitzel Farm. The Second Wave followed closely by the Third pushed on to meet a fair amount of opposition, mostly machine gun and rifle fire. A strong point in the shape of a huge dug-out with machine gun posts established was captured and yielded many prisoners and guns.

The enemy were now retreating to their next line but were quickly followed by the attackers who shot them down as they retreated, or took prisoner those who gave themselves up. Those that managed to escape would become casualties in the barrage.

Bethleem Farm and the Huts were ultimately reached and captured, these points yielding up many prisoners. The barrage now halted in front of where the storming troops were to consolidate. The knowledge that it would shelter them only for a certain time spurred them on to dig as quickly as possible a narrow, deep trench connecting up with shell holes.

The Battalion's final objective had now been won. A brilliant achievement which gave much satisfaction to those now holding the captured ground.

Major A. J. A. Maudsley, who had charge of forward operations, established Headquarters near Schnitzel Farm and directed all movements, also establishing a centre of communication. The forward signal party connected this position by 'phone to the Brigade cable head, which also connected with Battalion Battle Headquarters.

This line was successfully maintained throughout the remaining operations.

At ten minutes past three in the afternoon, incidentally, twelve hours to the very minute after zero hour, the 37th Battalion passed through the Black Line to capture the Green Line, but owing to heavy shelling by the enemy and the suffering of heavy casualties this Unit was ordered to retire and assist the 38th Battalion to consolidate their positions. It was reported that the enemy was preparing a counter attack which the 37th Battalion would not be strong enough to beat back. But owing to the good work of our artillery this counter attack failed to develop. At 3 a.m. on the following morning, Friday, 8th June, the 44th Battalion reinforced the two battalions and then passed on to successfully capture the Green Line.

These positions were held throughout the day, and in the early hours of Saturday morning came the cheering news of an early relief which took place just before dawn. As soon as the relieving troops appeared the men of the 38th Battalion were informed that they could independently make their way back to billets at Brune Gay by the easiest and safest route possible.

There was no need for this information to be repeated; rifles were snatched up and across country streamed a motley throng of weary, ragged, battle-stained men; a scene which made one think that the world's scarecrows had banded together from the four corners of the earth.

Thus ended the Battle of Messines, which instantly brought the Third Division into prominence, and placed its troops among the world's greatest fighters.

The Infantry accepted the praise they had won with a "Diggers" true modesty and passed it on to the artillery and machine gunners whose wonderful work alone had enabled them to perform their tasks in such a brilliant and successful manner.

Countless deeds of heroism had been performed and the following awards were won for the 38th Battalion.—

THE MILITARY CROSS.

Captain F. E. Fairweather, for courageous and able leadership of the Third Wave.

Captain R. E. Trebilcock, for gallant conduct and resourcefulness in commanding the Second Wave.

THE DISTINGUISHED CONDUCT MEDAL.

Sergt. P. L. Nihill, on 29th May, in the raid at Ploegsteert, brought in several wounded from the wire near the enemy trenches, and for this courageous act and for good work at Messines was awarded the Distinguished Conduct Medal.

Lance-Corporal G. B. Fullerton rushed a dugout, bayoneted several Boche and captured 30 prisoners.

Thirteen Military Medals were won as per appendix.

On the 12th June the Battalion moved by route march to hutments at Kortepyp. The distance of this place from Brune Gay was not great, and by midday all were settled down in the conveniently-placed and well-drained camp, where they stayed for a period of six days, during which time working parties were sent out daily to do repair work in the back area.

The next move was to Regina Camp, which consisted of a mixture of huts and tents in addition to a large deserted farm dwelling; the latter proving useful as a store, and for the accommodation of some troops.

The Battalion was not destined to stay long in one place. On account of military necessity which embraces so much, it is rarely found that a unit can remain in the same locality for much more than a week. This time it was not the will of the authorities that caused the shift.

The enemy, no doubt through aerial observation, knew exactly the location of the camp, and began to strafe it with long range, high velocity guns. The bombardments, however, were not intense, yet they were lively enough to cause the occupants of tents and huts alike to scamper to the open fields. Such is the method of the German gunners that once they have been directed on to a particular target they fire off their programme on to that spot, so the obvious thing to do is to move outside the area even away from cover.

As the result of these bombardments the Battalion was moved to another area.

The wisdom of this procedure was proved later when Regina Camp was almost demolished by artillery fire.

Although the distance to the new area was not great the operation was carried out in two stages. On the first night the Battalion rested in tents at Hillside Camp (Kortepyp). It was there that it witnessed for the first time a combined effort by enemy aeroplanes to destroy our long line of observation balloons, which on account of the continuous fine weather and consequent good visibility, was daily sent up to carry on silent though most important work. Two aeroplanes made the attempt and partly succeeded. Four balloons were shot down in flames in quick succession, and the occupants of the remaining three in that locality lost no time in jumping out into mid air with their parachutes. It was a unique sight to see at least a dozen men dangling in the air and slowly drifting with the breeze, to finally reach terra firma without having any choice as to where they would land.

On the following day the journey was continued and completed, so that on the 23rd June the Battalion found itself once again in tents in what was known as the Douve River Camp.

After the strenuous work in connection with the Messines operation the Battalion was due for a short spell, and it was decided that this period of rest should be enjoyed in the vicinity of Mont Kemmell; in fact, it was almost at the foot of the Mont that the Tenth Brigade settled down.

The River Douve flowed through the site; green hedges intersected the countryside and the presence of the ridge of high ground, or Mont, gave a little grandeur to what was, comparatively speaking a peaceful little spot.

Training of the less irksome nature was commenced and carried out with enthusiasm, as each battalion of the Brigade was anxious to appear at its best in the forthcoming Military Competition. Sports and cricket matches were organised; indeed, such relaxation was regarded almost as important as the military training. The Brigade cricket match was won by Brigade Headquarters team after a keen struggle with the 38th Battalion.

An eliminating contest was held on the same day to select the best complete Transport Section turnout to represent the Brigade in the Divisional Horse Show which was mooted for a fortnight later. This contest was won by the 38th Battalion by a narrow margin from the 40th Battalion. From this day until

July 8th, the day chosen for the Divisional meeting, horses, harness and vehicles were cleaned and polished to such an extent that when they appeared in the show-ring it was agreed that the turnout was as near perfection as possible. The judges had an easy task in deciding to award the prize for the best complete Transport turnout in the Division (a silver cup presented by Major-General Sir John Monash, G.O.C.) to the 38th Battalion. Other prizes won by the Transport Section were. —Pair of light draught horses and waggon (third prize, Driver S. McCorkill); pair of light draught mules and waggon (third prize, Lance-Corporal A. W. Landells); comic turnout (Q.M. Store staff). The Battalion's Transport Section created on that day (and has held ever since) a record second to none for turnout and general efficiency .

At these sports meetings and contests all ranks turned out to support in a vocal manner their own unit, and although their sporting instinct led them to applaud the brilliance of the opposing side, the esprit de corps, which was so strong in them. caused much satisfaction and pride when their own particular team came out victorious at the end of the day.

Thus the time was spent. Everyone forgot that the greatest of wars was still being continued.

Occasionally the distant muttering of guns, or a squadron of aeroplanes overhead might momentarily recall the latter fact.

When the time came again to get on with the more serious work the efficiency and the morale of the Battalion; in fact, of the whole Brigade, were at their best.

The next zone of activity of the Battalion was the support trenches at Messines, which were taken over from the 34th Battalion.

It was impossible to carry out the usual arrangements for the accommodation of the personnel, i.e., establishment in comfortable billets, for it must be remembered that this particular part of the country only a few months previously had suffered under our heavy bombardments, and in turn from the enemy retaliation.

However, by using the half-demolished pill-boxes, and cellars of ruined houses in the town of Messines; and by constructing a number of dugouts from material obtained from adjacent dumps, the Battalion was able to get enough shelter both from the elements and any observation of the enemy.

Each Company had a pill-box for its Company Headquarters around which trenches and dugouts were made, thus forming Company groups with Battalion Headquarters at a distance convenient for all Companies.

Working parties were required nightly by the front line Battalion for the purpose of constructing an adequate system of trenches for the defence of the locality. A good deal of this work devolved upon the 38th Battalion so that it was not long before all ranks became acquainted with such places as Septieme Barn, Blauen Molen, and Huns Walk.

The working parties generally finished their tasks by midnight and then retired to their dugouts to enjoy a well-earned rest. On two occasions, however, they were disturbed during the night by the whistling sounds of shells. On hearing these and the subsequent "plonk, plonk" of the low-explosions everyone realised that they were being subjected to a bombardment of gas shells, and at once donned their respirators. It was afterwards discovered that the particular species of gas used was of the Vesicent variety, commonly known as mustard gas. There was also a sprinkling of a shell called Blue Cross containing a substance, which, as the result of the explosion, assumed a powdered form and caused irritation to the nose and throat, and copious sneezing—hence sneezing gas.

These bombardments, although very annoying at the time, resulted in few casualties, but the blisters caused by contact of the skin with the mustard gas liquid for the time was the subject of much alarm both to the sufferers and the remaining troops. This anxiety was dispelled when it was subsequently observed that these new gases were not as formidable from a lethal point of view as their contemporaries phosgene, etc.

It was during the stay in this area that the Battalion lost Lieuts. Abbey and Wyndham who were killed on the morning of the 17th July. Unfortunately it was the last shell of a shoot which struck the shelter in which these two officers had sought cover. The loss did not end there. The same shell, in addition, accounted for the death of Sergeants Onions and Cunningham, and Pte. A. W. Marlow the last named being one of the family so well-known in the Battalion. All were buried next day by Chaplain Hayden in the Kandahar Cemetery, situated on the road to Neuve Eglise.

On the 20th July the Unit was relieved by the 40th Battalion and retired to a camp near Neuve Eglise, where it stayed for a period of fifteen days. This period may be described as practically uneventful. A long-range gun of huge calibre in the vicinity of the camp was the object of some interest to all ranks. The enemy also paid it some attention. but all attempts made by him to destroy it were unsuccessful.

Then a move was made in a rearward direction, and another prolonged stay was made at the Tankodrome Camp, near Dranoutre. This was another stage in the movement back to the rest area, and no time was lost in settling down to the preliminaries of training. By this time the spell of fine weather had broken, so there was a feeling of relief when orders came to evacuate the damp floored tents for a place somewhere west. Entrainment was carried out at Bailleul on the morning of August 14th, and by midday the Battalion, which had detrained at Wizernes, was route marching to its destination, Senlecques. which was reached after a long and strenuous journey that taxed to the limit, and in many cases over it, the staying powers of all concerned.

The Battalion arrived at Senlecques about midnight, when the kindly townsfolk turned out of their warm beds to welcome all, light fires. serve suppers, and see everyone comfortably settled down in billets.

Morning revealed a smiling landscape. Summer sunshine flooded green and gold fields where poppies nodded in the breeze. Birds sang gaily in the green-hedged lanes; rooks cawed and flopped about in the tops of tall poplars; while wayside brooks played a tiny tune for one's footsteps.

A mile across a green vale lay the village of La Calique, where "C" and "D" Companies were billeted.

After the shell-torn battlefields, and their attendant noises, how lovely and peaceful was this sunny little corner of France.

The warm-hearted inhabitants extended their friendship in a simple, irresistible manner, which quickly captivated the ever friendly Australian.

Happy days followed. When parade hours were over soldiers would be seen helping their French friends in the farming fields. Always there were willing hands to turn the well windlass and draw water for Marie or Hortense; and old toothless Grandmere would be assisted in the vegetable garden.

At night happy little companies gathered round the fires in the large farm kitchens and sipped coffee or wine. Perhaps "Madame" would have eggs for sale, when one of her saucepans would be requisitioned and all would sit down to an enjoyable supper ere retiring to billets.

In the neighborhood where the Transport Section was billeted lived a Frenchwoman who thought it would be wise to lock up her fowlhouse in case the members of the Transport should stray into it in search of eggs. A hole was cut in the door which allowed entrance for fowls only.

Every morning and evening Madame would unlock the door and collect her eggs. Naturally her caution interested the Transport people. Perhaps they rather resented her distrust in them. After a short consultation it was decided that a certain member of the Section should be detailed to daily relieve the fowlhouse of some of the eggs. Entrance to the hen nests could not be made by any man until the strong padlock had been broken, or the door knocked in. The day after arrangements had been made to raid the fowlhouse, a puzzled Frenchwoman found that the nests were nearly all devoid of eggs. The door and lock had not been tampered with; no one could have a key to fit the old-fashioned lock; and yet, somehow or other, the eggs had been taken. Every day the nests contained a few odd eggs instead of about two dozen. Madame might fortify the door with heavy cart chains and declare the men of the Transport to be "brigandes" (without being able to prove that they were) and still the eggs mysteriously disappeared.

When Madame was busily working in an adjacent field, Jacko, the Transport mascot, with all a monkey's cunning, would sneak in through the hole cut in the door and hand out the eggs to his soldier comrades.

When the Transport Section left Senecques Madame was delighted and amazed at the generosity of the men who presented her with a bundle of franc notes.

It was the price of the stolen eggs.

The six weeks period of rest will ever be remembered as one of the happiest times the Battalion had in France. Five kilomentres distant from billets was the fine town of Desvres. One of the attractions of the town was a large swimming bath at the Potteries. This bath measured 50ft by 28ft by 6ft and was always full of warm water.

Roads leading out from Senlecques wound their way through golden fields and twisted down into green valleys. The hours of training were made pleasant by delightful surroundings; and route marches along flower-flanked roads and shady lanes were thoroughly enjoyed. Special training for a big battle in the near future was carried out when the 38th Battalion met the sister battalions of the Tenth Brigade, which were billeted in neighboring townships.

An amusing incident (which would, no doubt, have pleased certain harsh critics of the Australian Army who state that we are an undisciplined lot) occurred during a practise field operation by the Tenth Brigade. Orders were given that strict silence be observed. The Brigade was strictly obeying the order when a hare rushed in among the ranks. This chance of sport proved too much of a test to keep silence and order. The ranks broke, and steel hats whizzed through the air as the bewildered hare dodged in and out among his pursuers. The chase was fast and furious. Finally, the hare was killed by a barrage of steel hats.

On the 22nd September the Third Division was inspected by the Commander-in-Chief, Field Marshall Sir Douglas Haig. The inspection took place in a field near Drionville.

The weather was good, and the Division formed up in battalions en masse presented a fine military spectacle. A party of Red Cross sisters witnessed the inspection, and the visitors were afterwards entertained by the Battalion.

The Unit bade farewell to Senlecques and La Calique on Sept. 25th, and for four days marched by easy stages via Assinghem, Lynde and Terdeghem to a camp in the neighborhood of Winnizeele.

On the 2nd of October the Battalion proceeded by motor buses to Vlarmertinghe, and marched to a bivouac area east of Ypres on the right of Ypres-Zonnebeke road.

Early in September, 1917, the fighting at Ypres had begun. This series of operations east of the town, lasting until well on in the month of November, was called the Third Battle of Ypres. Every week after careful artillery preparation a fresh attack was launched and new ground won; and it was in two of these attacks—phases of the great battle, as they were called—the 38th Battalion took a prominent part.

On the night of October 2/3, as already mentioned, the Battalion bivouacked under the hedge of a field just east of the town, and on the right of the Ypres-Zonnebeke road. It rained during the night and those who had neglected to take precautions against the weather found themselves wet through when dawn arrived. However, the day of the 3rd was fine, and the sun, with the aid of fires, soon made amends for the state of the weather experienced during the night. On this day final preparations were made for the coming attack. Officers were busy gathering information about the operation and at the first opportunity passing it on to all concerned. N.C.O.'s were employed in issuing the additional battle equipment, such as flares, S.O.S. signal rockets, extra water bottles and the many other articles so necessary for the attacking troops. All officers and a proportion of N.C.O.'s and men (chiefly scouts) spent half the day in a reconnaissance of the approach route and the area to be assaulted, the former, by the way, not being finally completed until late in the afternoon. The place of assembly and the various land marks, so necessary for the maintenance of direction, were distinctly visible through field glasses, their positions being verified on the spot by reference to the maps which had been liberally supplied.

It was during these expeditions before the battle that one got an insight into some of the methods of organisation and saw the necessity of careful and thorough preparation of all details. The roads were necessarily crammed full of vehicles of all kinds, motor and horse, pack mules laden with shells and ammunition; equestrians from the rank of Major-General down to Private; guns drawn both by tractor and horse; and, finally, the small bodies of men on foot threading their way through the traffic. One wondered how any movement at all was possible with such apparent over-crowding. Nevertheless, it was achieved and much credit is due to those responsible for traffic control and road repair, and all other personnel employed to assist in the passage of all arms along the roads.

The 10th Brigade was allotted a frontage of just over 500 yards for the attack. On the right the 11th Brigade had a similar frontage, whilst a New Zealand Brigade was made responsible for the ground on the immediate left.

The order for the attack within the 10th Brigade was 37th, 38th, 39th, and 40th Battalions, and the system to be employed was the leap frog method. By this it is meant that the 37th Battalion captured the first objective, the 38th the second and so on, the 40th being the rear Battalion, had the furthest objective—a distance of about 2000 yards.

The various companies of the Battalion were disposed in the following order:—First Wave, two platoons of C Company (Captain Selleck) left, and two platoons of D Company (Captain Orchard) right, followed by B Company (Captain E. F. Moore) as moppers up. Second Wave: Remainder of C and D Companies; A Company (Captain Dench) in rear as reserve Company.

The objective was described as "C.S", actually a line running N.W. and S.E. in front of Bordeaux and Springfield Farms.

Tentative Headquarters for the Brigade and the various Battalions were established in the various concrete dug-outs, as near as possible to the jumping-off place, then later were moved forward and established in the dugouts allotted to them just in rear of their Units. It happened that the 38th Battalion Headquarters pill-box (Mitchell Farm) was still full of and surrounded by dead Germans, making the place uninhabitable so that Major Hurry, who was in command, together with his staff were obliged to take possession of Square Farm for their temporary Headquarters.

V.—HILL 63 AND PLOEGSTEERT WOOD.

VI.—LILLE GATE, YPRES.

VII.—A BIG CRATER AT YPRES.

VIII.—FLANDERS MUD.

Zero hour was fixed at 6 a.m. on the morning of the 4th. As the whole Brigade had to use the one avenue of approach—"K" track—the leading Battalion for the attack had to move off at an hour sufficiently early to allow the rear Battalion to be in position in ample time.

The approach march commenced without a hitch, the 38th following the 37th in single file along the duckboards of the track. Then came the other two Battalions, also in single file. Thus it might be said that the whole Brigade was in single file, though it is probable that the front Battalion was getting into position before the rear Unit had actually left its quarters.

The desultory shelling which was in progress increased in intensity as the troops approached the Assembly ground. Casualties were inevitable, still the gaps were closed and the flood of manhood pressed on, while the stretcher-bearers silently performed their duty to those who were forced by wounds to fall out. Everybody was anxious to push on, but it was apparent that there would be some little delay to allow each Company in succession to assume its correct formation and proper position. However, by midnight the 38th Battalion was reposing in shell holes along the latter and the shelling had died down a little. Evidently the enemy had not noticed anything unusual happening. Even our own artillery, which had been carrying out its covering bombardment, now that the necessity for such was over, closed down to enjoy a short rest before the big event.

It must not be thought, however, that firing had wholly ceased. Such a display of inactivity on the part of the British gunners would at once give an indication to a shrewd enemy that something was "in the wind."

At about 5.30 a.m. observers noticed on the right a display of lights of all colors, and it was at once thought that the enemy had perceived us. This impression was confirmed as the alarm spread along the whole front. An enemy barrage was put down, but there was nothing for us but to sit fast and endure it, and pray for the hands of the clock to move faster towards zero hour.

At last it came! A sigh of relief escaped from every mouth as each man got up to follow the leading waves. Our barrage was splendid, and the immediate and almost complete silence of the Boche guns gave a clear indication that those of our guns responsible for counter battery work were carrying out their job to perfection.

The 38th Battalion followed close upon the heels of the 37th Battalion, and all obstacles were speedily overcome. On the left practically the only opposition came from a single machine gun post, which was quickly subdued by our men in conjunction with the New Zealanders. In the centre a Machine Gun post at Israel House gave trouble for a time, but it in its turn received its quietus. The concrete pill-boxes about Judah House and Springfield Farm caused a little anxiety and delay. The capture of these strong posts yielded several machine guns and about 150 prisoners. In almost every case the opposition was overcome by working around to the rear of the obstacle and throwing in a "P" bomb or Mills grenade as an inducement to the occupants to come up and "Kamarade."

Generally speaking, our men kept so close to the barrage that they were upon the enemy before he had time to recover from its effects.

The Battalion's objective was reached by 7.30 a.m. and consolidation immediately began under the direction of Capt. W. H. Orchard, who found himself in charge of the attacking troops after the death of Captain E. F. Moore and the retirement, through wounds, of Captain H. F. Selleck. It was the efficient manner in which he (Captain Orchard) carried out his task of reorganisation, and his cheerfulness under depressing circumstances that earned for him the Military Cross.

By this time Battalion Headquarters had reached Judah House and touch was immediately established with the forward troops by means of runner and telephone.

At 9.39 a.m. an enemy aeroplane flew low over the line but apparently failed to locate it, as the hostile artillery was at no time very accurate.

Early in the afternoon a platoon of "D" Company (No. 15) was sent forward to reinforce the 39th Battalion, and one Company of 150 men was organised to be ready to move forward at a moment's notice to assist in a contemplated further advance.

On the night of October 5/6, at 9 p.m., the enemy put down a heavy box barrage, which, however, caused comparatively few casualties. Several times during the night our S.O.S. signals were sent up from the front line and the response by our artillery was wonderfully prompt.

On one occasion—the last—when the signal was sent up the batteries of machine guns which had been established in rear as an additional support to the artillery opened fire alone. This was sufficient in itself to check any attempt at counter attack.

That same night the Battalion was relieved by the 28th Manchesters and marched through Ypres to hutments in the neighborhood of Vlamentinghe, which were reached by 6.30 on the morning of October 6th. An excellent breakfast had been prepared, and after having supplied the wants of the "inner man" all ranks settled down, and soon the misery of the mud and the fury of the battle were forgotten, being lost in deep slumbers, all the more enjoyable because of the absence of any rest whatever during the preceding three days.

The Casualties for the operation were:—

	Killed.	Wound.	Missing.	Total.
Officers	1	1	0	2
Other Ranks	33	142	7	182
	34	143	7	184

The total personnel engaged was approximately 650, so that the percentage of casualties, which works out at 29 can be regarded as low; wheras the experience gained by all ranks, together with the amount of ground won from, and damage inflicted on, the enemy was considerable; so great, in fact, that, although casualties are inevitable even though regrettable, the balance of profit was much to the Battalion's credit.

Prisoners captured by us amounted to about 300. Major G. Hurry (now Lieut.-Colonel), who as already mentioned was in command of the Battalion, was awarded the D.S.O. He showed a fine example to all ranks and fought his Battalion with great skill, contributing largely towards the success of the operation.

The courage and devotion to duty displayed by Sergeant J. S. Shilliday (now Lieut.) and Lance-Corpl. A. A. G. Bright, earned for each the D.C.M.

Thirteen Military Medals were won by the Battalion during the operation.

For a few days following the relief of the Battalion reorganisation was speedily carried out. Platoons had to be made up to strength for further fighting, and for this purpose the nucleus personnel which had retired to Morbecque was absorbed. Lost or battle-worn equipment was immediately replaced, and in addition, a fresh issue of battle supplies left no one in doubt as to whether the Battalion would participate in further fighting.

On October 10th the hutments at Vlamertinghe were vacated and the Unit marched to a bivouac known as Hussar Farm. Immediately on arrival all ranks set to work on the construction of temporary shelters and in less than two hours, what was once a bare strip of land was converted into a veritable township sheltering between 600 to 700 men.

The date of the next attack was fixed at October 12th and as on the previous occasion, everyone had been busy in the preparations for the event. Lieut.-Colonel C. H. Davis, D.S.O., had resumed command, whilst Major Hurry was temporarily detached for Divisional duty.

Arrangements up to date were satisfactory, though it was recognised that as the ground to be covered was low-lying, and as so much rain had fallen the conditions would be such as to test the grit and doggedness of the storming troops to the utmost.

The 38th Battalion was allotted the third or final objective —a line beyond the village of Passchendaele. A New Zealand Brigade and the 9th Australian Infantry Brigade were allotted the ground respectively on our left and right. At 10.45 pm. on the night of the 11/12. The approach march was begun. Soon after entering "K" track enemy shell fire was encountered.

This shelling continued intermittently until the assembly lines were reached making our casualties rather considerable, especially near the junction of "K" track and the sunken road.

In addition, gas shells fell on the low-lying ground northeast of Judah House, but owing to the high velocity of the wind, the effect was not marked.

By 3 a.m. the Battalion had formed up on its tapes in the following order:—

Two platoons of "A" Company (Captain Trebilcock) right, plus two platoons of "B" Company (Captain Latchford) left, formed the First Wave; "D" Company (Lieut. Maxwell) were behind as "moppers up"; the remaining platoons of "A" and "B" Companies formed the Second Wave. "C" Company (Lieut. Herring) as "moppers up" in rear.

While waiting for zero hour the enemy shelling was acute and many casualties resulted, so that by zero hour the Battalion had been weakened considerably in numbers; and those who had survived had already received a severe handling.

The advance was commenced in rear of the 40th Battalion, but soon heavy machine gun fire was encountered from the left (Bellevue). One party, under Lieutenant Munday, worked its way across the Rave Beek and cleared three pill boxes, but was eventually stopped by heavy rifle and machine gun fire. They dug in where they stood, and next night rejoined the main body, which, in the meantime, had advanced to the Red Line, where the 38th was amalgamated with the remnants of the 37th and 40th Battalions. Casualties had been so severe that further advance was impossible, especially as the New Zealand troops on our left, through encountering belts of uncut wire, and suffering enormous casualties had failed to get forward. Consequently Major Giblin (40th Batt.) Senior Officer present, ordered a withdrawal to approximately the jumping-off line where consolidation was completed by 3 p.m.. In conjunction with the remainder of the Brigade the 38th Battalion held this line until relieved on the night of 13/14 by the 41st Battalion A.I.F., when the Battalion moved to bivouacs again at Hussar Farm.

During the operation the Battalion Battle Headquarters was established in a pill box in Berlin Wood, as also was the Regimental Aid Post and Quartermaster's Store. Transport personnel and other details were camped in a field on the right of the Ypres-Zonnebeke road.

Although actually out of the battle area this camp during the progress of the fight received a good deal of attention from the enemy long-range high velocity guns, and hostile aeroplanes which paid a nightly visit to the spot.

Our casualties during the operation were very numerous. The following officers were put completely out of action (i.e., killed or missing):—Killed: Lieuts. Robinson, Maxwell, Matthews, Morrison, Marshall. Missing: Lieut. McKenzie.

The following is a summary of the casualties:—

	Killed.	Missing.	Wound.	Total.
Officers	5	1	7	13
Other Ranks	6	99	263	368
	11	100	270	381

The percentage of casualties to the number engaged was 62, being the highest of any operation carried out by the Battalion.

Despite the failure of the operation many deeds of heroism were performed, the most notable on this occasion being the Distinguished Service Order won by Captain G. V. Davies, the Battalion Medical Officer.

The following is the quotation from the A.I.F. List No. 214:—"For conspicuous gallantry and devotion to duty in going forward through an intense barrage and establishing a Regimental Aid Post in an advanced position, remaining on duty continuously for fifty-four hours, often working in the open under heavy fire. When the Aid Post was hit by a shell he extricated a man who was buried and continued his work. He remained for fifteen hours after the Battalion was relieved till the last man was carried to safety, and set a magnificent example to all."

A Military Cross was awarded to Capt. Latchford for conspicuous gallantry and devotion to duty, in reorganising the Battalion after it had suffered heavy casualties. In addition, ten Military Medals were awarded for good work in both operations (4th and 12th).

During the whole of the operations at Ypres and Passchendaele more so than during any other period of the Battalion's history, the one awful aspect which constantly presented itself was that of mud!

As far as the eye could see, the whole countryside was pock-marked with hundreds of thousands of shell holes of all shapes and sizes, and not the slightest sign of vegetation was to be seen anywhere, the earth having been completely churned up.

The shells had fallen so constantly and frequently that eventually the existing holes had been, and were being, torn open afresh and made deeper and larger than before. These shell holes through soakage rapidly filled with water and conditions were accentuated by the almost continual rain which descended daily over this shattered area.

There was something terribly sinister and terrifying about the mud of the Ypres and Passchendaele battlefields. Men knew that if they fell wounded in one of those gaping holes they stood little change of being rescued, that they would probably be suffocated in the thick glutinous substance which gripped everything which touched it like the tentacles of a giant octopus seizing upon its prey. And this is actually what happened to many a brave man—German as well as British. And yet, despite everything, our men labored on with grim set faces and that indomitable spirit which eventually won us the war. And the animals were almost as dogged in their persistence.

Pack horses and mules carrying forward ammunition, engineering supplies and rations would constantly fall into and sink—sometimes out of sight—in the terrible mud of the shell holes. Hours would be spent by the faithful drivers in an endeavor to rescue their helpless beasts, but very often the animals were so helplessly bogged that there was no alternative but to put an end to their struggles and torture by a revolver or rifle bullet.

The guns had to be supported on specially constructed platform to prevent them sinking. When the time came to follow the advancing infantry the artillerymen performed almost superhuman feats, but even then not without guns and teams becoming hopelessly bogged when they got off their specially prepared tracks.

During the Battalion's operations at Ypres and Passchendaele it was quite a common occurrence for the men to sink to their thighs and waists into the soft, slimy mud, which drew one down, down, for ever downward like some live thing. But still they endured and achieved what appeared almost impossible and bore their trials with a joke and a smile upon their faces. And a word here for the heroic stretcher-bearers will not be out of place. To carry a wounded man from the front line to the R.A.P. was a terrible undertaking. The distance to be covered was less than a thousand yards, but it took six men four, five and even six hours to do the trip. Many a helplessly wounded man through some of his bearers falling or sinking into a shell hole, would roll off the stretcher and feel himself being sucked down—and all this under constant enemy shell fire. Truly the heroic deeds performed at Ypres and Passchendaele have never been excelled!

After strenuous fighting under such adverse conditions the Third Division was withdrawn for a rest. The 38th Battalion left the battle area for the purpose of embussing at a point somewhere in the neighborhood of Vlamerringe. It was necessary to pass through Ypres, and it was in the centre of that town where further trouble was met. The enemy was shelling the place with heavy long-range guns. Headquarters and "A" Company, who were in the lead received the full force of a shell which killed Lieut. Kirkbride, Reg. Sergeant-Major Rust and others. Captain Trebilcock and others were wounded. Twenty-three casualties were caused altogether. In addition many records were destroyed, including most of "A" Company's official records.

The remaining Companies got through without casualties, and it was not long before the Battalion (all that were left) had started on their journey away from the scene of so much desolation and ruin.

* * * *

CHAPTER IV.

WARNETON TO THE SOMME.

On the 15th October the Battalion moved by motor buses to Senlecques, and was again warmly welcomed by its old friends. But many soldier faces were missed by the good French folk, who, with tear-filled eyes listened to the quietly-told story of "Billy's" or "Jack's" death on the battlefield of Ypres.

Once again the Battalion settled down to enjoy several happy weeks in this neighborhood.

Summer had passed and Autumn was painting trees and hedges with her gay brush. Training was carried out and kit inspections were held when shortages of clothing and equipment were replaced.

When the time came to again move up towards the line the Battalion was greatly refreshed by this restful period.

Moving by motor bus to the La Motte area on November 10th the Unit billeted for the night at Verte Rue and Cordescure, and on the following day marched to Noote Boom in the Vieux Berquin area. Hollybeque Farm was reached on the 12th.

After twenty-four hours' rest the Battalion moved on to relieve the Sherwood Foresters in the left battalion sector of Warneton sector.

The first stage of the journey up to the line was an easy one by rail from the Railhead Dump at Steinwerok Station to Hyde Park Corner. But shortly after leaving the latter place the Battalion's troubles began. The night was particularly dark, and duckboard tracks sadly needed repairing. The railway track along which Captain W. H. Orchard led "D" Company was in a vile condition. The continuous marching of troops along it had worn deep hollows in between the sleepers, and these were full of mud and water into which "D" Company splashed.

On arrival at the trenches the Battalion was reminded of the muddy, water-logged defences of Houplines. The Warneton trenches were in a fearful condition owing to bad weather, and the previous occupants neglecting to make them habitable.

The eight days spent in the line were fairly quiet. During this time the trenches were overhauled, and when on the 21st November the Unit was relieved by the 40th Battalion there was a marked improvement in the defences.

The Battalion retired to hutments at Romarin as a reserve battalion. Here eight pleasant days were spent in a comfortable camp.

The surrounding country, despite its flatness, was not unpicturesque. Here and there quaint old windmills stood out against the sky with their red sails turning around and around to the breezes. The open fields were dotted with red-roofed houses, and the main roads could be traced by their avenues of stately trees.

Working parties were daily employed unloading trucks of shells at ammunition dumps, and on various jobs in the forward area. A network of light railway lines was spread over the country, and busy little engines continually hauled loads of ammunition, building material, etc along to the various dumps, and puffed their way through Ploegsteert Wood to within a mile of the line. Tram tracks connected with the railway and ran right up the trenches through a wilderness of shell holes. These tracks were often shelled by the enemy and many a working or ration party experienced exciting times while pushing the hand-trucks along these bumpy but serviceable lines.

The puffing of engines and the rumbling of trucks could be clearly heard by the enemy. On clear, frosty nights it must have seemed to him that the busy little engines would come puffing along into his trenches.

The Battalion again took over the Warneton sector on November 29th. This time the enemy made things a little livelier. His trench mortars pounded the defences from time to time. Our Artillery constantly "strafed" him, with the usual result—retaliation.

A great source of annoyance was the Warneton Tower. which the enemy used for purposes of observation. This building was clearly visible from the trenches and stood out above the town. The artilllery continually "strafed" it, but it seemed to defy destruction.

From the tower the enemy commanded a splendid view of the area and could watch any movement on the high ground on the outskirts of Ploegsteert Wood. It was not until three months later that it was destroyed by a naval gun which was commissioned to hurl tons of iron and high explosive at it.

Passing through Ploegsteert Wood, now denuded of foliage by Winter, and lacerated by enemy bombardments, one's thoughts went back to the warm, sunny days of the month of May, when Spring had glorified the flower-filled aisles of the wood. Here was a striking illustration of the ugliness of war; shattered trees, a charred stump where once a spreading chestnut had held up a canopy of green leaves and graceful pink blossoms; a giant oak split in two by half a ton of iron; deep ugly gashes in the earth; grasses and leaves withered by deadly gases. One of Nature's choicest works converted into an unlovely wilderness.

On the 6th December the 38th Battalion was relieved by its old friends of the 40th Battalion and retired to Red Lodge, about a mile and a half behind the line. Here it lived in dugouts excavated in the side of a hill; snug little homes, lit up with electric light and fitted with bunks.

The next move was to Aldershot Camp on the Waterloo Road, a mile behind the town of Neuve Eglise, where the Battalion was accommodated in hutments for five days and on the 20th December retired to Hollebeke Camp (Jesus Farm) in the Steinwerch area. Here the Battalion spent its second Christmas in France.

The weather was bitterly cold. Heavy frosts and snow covered the land with cold, white garments; but around blazing fires, when the cold was forgotten, Christmas was merrily celebrated. The Battalion cooks served up a fine Christmas dinner, which was thoroughly enjoyed.

Perhaps some of the hardest workers in the Battalion were the cooks. Up in the coldest hours of the morning, long before dawn, they toiled away until midnight. When the Battalion was in the line meals had to be prepared at all hours and often under great difficulties and danger, but the cooks never failed under the most trying circumstances to provide good hot meals. Great praise is due to them for their splendid work. Good meals mean contented men; well-fed soldiers are fighters. The 38th Battalion cooks helped to win for their Unit fame and glory.

The Hun was now boasting to the world that he would shortly sweep through Belgium and France with his "irresistible storm-troops" which he stated would shortly be massed for this onward rush. The Kaiser again adopted his favorite pastime of making wildly patriotic speeches, extracts of which almost daily appeared in the world's newspapers. According to the Hun the war would be quickly brought to a finish by his great onward rush. Although his boasting failed to alarm the Allies every precaution was taken to meet the threatened attack. Reconnoitring parties from all Units proceeded to certain areas, where, slightly in rear of the line, defences had been prepared in case the enemy should break through.

A party of officers and N.C.O.'s of the 38th Battalion reconnoitred the positions allotted to the Unit in the neighborhood of Le Bizet. This work proved very interesting for it entailed careful study of the features of the country. In case of an enemy attack the Battalion would immediately go forward and occupy these selected positions, led there by those who had gained a thorough knowledge of the area.

Rations and water were stored close to the defences, and every military necessity was gone into and arranged for with great care and thoroughness.

On the last day of the year the Battalion returned to Aldershot Camp, where it remained until the 27th January. The New Year ushered in stormy weather, which often interrupted the work of training. Heavy rains flooded the camp for two days, and working parties had a very miserable time. Following the rain came heavy frosts and snow. The ground became frozen to a depth of two feet. Twelve months ere this a system of water pipes had been laid down in the neighborhood by engineers. The pipes were only eighteen inches underground with the result that the water in them froze. The Battalion had the contract of taking them up and burying them at a depth of five feet. Another unpleasant contract was digging cable trenches. Owing to the heavy rains the low-lying ground was in a waterlogged condition, the result being that water oozed into the trenches as they were dug. Gumboots had to be worn for the water often came up above one's knees. Then, again, where the ground was not quite so wet the walls of the trenches had a nasty trick of falling in, so that a man's daily task was often doubled. Towards the end of this stay at Aldershot Camp the weather became quite pleasant, when bright, sunny days had a cheering effect upon everyone.

It was almost like a touch of Spring; the big "sausage" balloons floated lazily up in the sunshine and aeroplanes droned overhead, looking like silver dragon flies. Towards evening enemy 'planes would sometimes venture over to attack the balloons. Immediately they were sighted the "Archies," or antiaircraft guns would surround the balloons with a protecting curtain of shrapnel, which the Boche would not venture to penetrate. Occasionally the enemy's night bombing 'planes would pay the neighborhood a visit, when searchlights for miles around would sweep the heavens and once they fastened on an enemy 'plane it received a warm reception. The red flashes of bursting "Archies" would wink about the 'plane, and phosphorus, or Tracer bullets, would stream up through the night like long lines of fireflies.

Captain A. Fraser, with a fine record of good work, was on January 1 1918 awarded the Military Cross. Captain Fraser had served in Gallipoli, where he was wounded. Returning to

Australia for a short time, he joined the 38th Battalion as Adjutant and was finally, in February, 1919, promoted to command the Unit. Captain Fraser was one of a few who served continually with the Unit during its sojourn in France.

On this date Lance-Corporal F. J. Perry was awarded the Distinguished Conduct Medal for a continuous record of good work as a scout.

In accordance with Battalion Order No. 57 the Unit relieved the 23rd Battalion A.I.F. in the Warneton Sector on January 27th. The relief was complete at 9.15 p.m. The Battalion moved from Aldershot lines to Connaught Siding, thence by light railway to Hyde Park Corner, from where it once again trudged along the duckboards up to the trenches. The relief passed without incident, some of the members of the 23rd Battalion being heard to remark that it was the quickest relief they had ever had.

The dispositions of the Battalion were as follows:—In the front line were two platoons of "A" Company and two platoons of "C" Company. The remainder of "A" and "C" Companies were in close support; "B" Company was in support in Grey Trench, and "D" Company in reserve in the Catacombs. B.H.Q. was established in an old pill box against the subsidiary line. The Quartermaster's Store and the Transport Section were at Antrim Lines and Romarin Siding.

Owing to the bad weather experienced early in the month the trenches were in a bad state. Useful Lane (a communication trench) despite its name was in places impassable. Along Wally Support and River Lane the mud was of such a sticky nature that it was difficult to drag one's feet out of it. The front line was in the same condition.

During the stay in the trenches the weather was fine and remarkably mild thus making it possible for the defences to be put in fair condition. The enemy's artillery fire was almost as mild as the weather, but his trench mortars were fairly active.

On being relieved on the 4th February the Battalion again moved to Red Lodge.

Coming out from the line, weary, loaded with gear, and plastered with mud, a light shining out on the Messines Road drew one like a magnet to an old tin shanty.

Here the Y.M.C.A. toilers had prepared steaming cocoa which was greedily drunk from condensed milk tins. Biscuits and cigarettes were handed out, and trudging on again, with the glowing end of a "fag" illuminating the tip of his nose, many a "digger" muttered, "Good old Y. Emma!"

At Red Lodge everyone enjoyed the luxury of a hot bath and a change of clothing, both of which were badly needed after spending eight days in muddy trenches

It was not a time of rest, for all available men were needed for working parties and kept busily employed on various jobs from daylight to dark.

Towards the end of January (23rd) whilst the Battalion was stationed at Aldershot Camp (Neuve Eglise) a party of five officers and 100 other ranks was selected to commence training with a view of raiding the enemy during a subsequent period of duty in the line in front of Warneton. This party, together with a similar number from the 37th Battalion, went to Romney Camp, near Romarin, where, under Captain Fairweather, M.C. (38th) they commenced training in earnest for the task before them. Smartness in turnout and in drill was insisted upon from the outset; physical training and bayonet fighting were made prominent features; whilst careful attention was paid to such special subjects as hand and rifle bombing, and also anti-gas training.

Practice in crossing wire both by day and night was given; and later on the intended raid was performed more than once over a model which was an exact replica of the enemy's trenches. Each night a proportion of officers and men went forward to the line as reconnoitring patrols, so that, by the day of the raid, every man was fully acquainted with the obstacles likely to be encountered, and had a good idea of the features of the ground over which he would be working.

A Special Party, under Lieut. Barker, was detailed to receive instructions in the handling of dummy figures, which were to be used to deceive the enemy as to the exact point of the real attack, thereby assisting the surprise effect and causing the dispersal of the enemy retaliatory fire. This body was styled the "Chinese Party," and probably derives its name from the unprogressive nature of its intended job.

The remaining members were divided mainly into two assaulting teams, operating respectively on the North and on the South of the road leading into Warneton. Each of these teams was divided into eight separate parties; and to each of these sixteen parties was assigned a definite rule, task and objective. The total duration of our occupation of the enemy's position was to be 26 minutes, and the total penetration, measured from his front line, 250 yards on a total frontage of 500 yards. The left team was comprised of 38th Battalion men, led by Lieutenants Churchill, Eason and Schlitz (C.O left Assault) and the right team was made up from the 37th Battalion personnel.

Whilst all these preparations were in progress arrangements were being made by the Artillery and Machine Gun Company and Trench Mortar Battery to afford as much assistance as possible to the raiders. Programmes for the barrage (Artilery and Machine Gun), counter battery work with gas and harassing and covering fire were drawn up; and on "X" day—the day prior to the raid—the wire was cut at various points along our own Divisional front and that of the neighboring Division on the north. The Lewis Guns in the line prevented any repair to such gaps, and on the morning of "Z" day, as an extra precaution, a further shoot by Trench Mortars was arranged. The thoroughness with which the arrangements for co-operation of all arms were made is exemplified in the following account of the details concerning them.—

"The Artillery will carry out an advancing barrage which will rest 100 yards beyond the furthermost point of penetration and be maintained there until the close of the operation. In addition the Reinforcing Brigade will keep under fire the enemy's front line to the northward of the point of attack. The Artillery of the left flank Division will carry out a division bombardment whilst Corps heavy artillery will bombard trench inter-sections, which the enemy is likely to reinforce. Rear targets will also be engaged.

In addition the 10th Machine Gun Company and the 10th Trench Mortar Battery will carry out such work as an additional barrage, covering fire and engaging such targets by harassing fire as might be the assembly places or approach routes for assisting enemy troops."

The arrangements made for the maintenance of communication were such that information and reports were assured. Telephone lines were to be laid between the officer in charge of the raid and the two officers in charge of Assault, stationed under the enemy's parapet.

In the event of these being cut, runners had to be substituted. A power buzzer was installed, so that in the event of a break in the wire in rear, messages could be sent without the employment of the slow method—runners.

At 5.30 p.m. on "Z" night the raiders left Camp, entrained at Connaught Siding (light railway), detrained at Racine Dump, and then moved by Vancouver Track to Au Chasseur Cabaret, thence overland to the factory by a taped route. By 9.56 p.m. the parties had assembled in two lines of single rank with a distance of 30 yards between lines, in the order in which they were to enter the enemy's trenches. So far, they had suffered no interference. Friendly patrols were operating in No Man's Land to prevent any enemy observation.

All was quiet until, punctually at 10 p.m., the barrage came down. The raiding parties paused for a full minute whilst the "Chinese Party", who were lying down 400 yards to the north, pulled the cords which raised the silhouette figures from the ground. The trick had succeeded. Intense enemy fire, Machine Gun and Artillery, was directed on to the dummy figures. Then at zero (plus one minute) the parties moved forward to the attack through the gaps marked on the map A and K respectively. The passage through the wire was easy, but the first opposition came early, for during the first minute of the hurricane bombardment, the Boche had moved forward from his own trenches to a zone of safety. There they met our advancing parties full of dash, spirit and determination. In a short space of time this resistance was overcome, and at least 30 of the enemy were killed and some taken prisoner.

The left assaulting team (38th) met practically no opposition in the front line, but strong resistance in the second line, where they found a number of dugouts affording protection to the defending troops. They demolished three of these, so that with the two which were already destroyed by artillery fire, a considerable amount of damage was inflicted.

At 10.24 two minutes before the time for withdrawal—a strong counter attack developed along the Warneton road, but this was repulsed by rifle and Machine Gun fire, and the withdrawal of our troops was thereby covered. The return journey was made via The Factory, Vancouver Track to Racine Dump,

HISTORY OF 38th BATTALION, A.I.F.

where the party entrained for Connaught Siding, thence home to billets again at Romney Camp, to enjoy a hot meal which had been prepared for them.

The result of the raid cannot be too highly estimated. When one comes to consider the fact that at least 100 of the enemy garrison had been killed (including one Company Commander). 33 taken prisoner, and much booty—three machine guns, one trench mortar and medical equipment)—captured, together with the amount of material damage inflicted he cannot but come to the conclusion that the operation ranks as a brilliant success; in fact, it is justly claimed that this raid was the most successful ever carried out by the 38th Battalion. The results obtained by our men in the face of strong opposition by a resolute enemy must compare favorably with any similar operation throughout the Division, even in the whole Australian Corps.

Our casualties (38th Battalion), totalled six, making a percentage to the number engaged of about 5.6.

Lieutenants Schlitz and Churchill were each awarded a Military Cross for splendid work in the operation. In addition the names of Pte. R. L. M. Gelly, Cpl. J. Wallace, Pte. J. Grant and E. C. Umbers figured in the list of awards for Military Medals for specially good work.

Captain F. E. Fairweather, M.C., who had charge of the operation from the commencement of the training until the final report, proved once again, by his thoroughness, courage and skill, that he was a soldier of the highest quality and a most successful leader of men.

The Warneton sector was again taken over on February 12th, when the 40th Battalion was relieved.

The relief passed without incident, and was complete at 8.15 p.m. The trenches were in a considerably better condition, although there was a good deal of water in the front line. the communication trenches and supports were dry. The Division had seriously undertaken the work of improving the sector, large parties of men being employed nightly under the supervision of engineers and pioneers.

On the night of the 18th the enemy put down a heavy barrage on the front, support, and communication trenches. This was repeated at 2.15 a.m., 2.30, 4 and 5 o'clock. The trenches were only slightly damaged, and casualties were light, two men being wounded.

During the stay in the trenches the weather remained remarkably fine, and an immense amount of work was done, so that by the time the Battalion was relieved it was possible to tour the whole of the front line wearing only ankle boots.

The relief took place on February 19th, when the Unit retired to the Catacombs, Hyde Park Corner, as a support Battalion.

The Catacombs was really an underground city, a network of tunnels under a hill. These subterranean passages were fitted out to accommodate about 1500 men, and here one could rest in peace, and laugh at shells and bombs. Lit up by electricity and fitted with bunks the Catacombs was quite a comfortable place of abode.

On the 24th of the month the Battalion moved to "A" Camp, Kortepyp.

The long-threatened attack by the Boche was expected at any time and a Corps line was being garrisoned by A.I.F. Units.

The whole of "D" Company and selected parties from other Companies of the Battalion took over ten (10) posts in this line from February 24th until the Unit moved to billets in the Lumbres area on 4th March, when the Third Division was due for a rest.

Arriving at Lumbres by train at nightfall the Battalion marched to billets several miles out of the town; B.H.Q. and "A" Company proceeded to Ardenis-lez Sheninghem, and "B", "C" and "D" Companies to Affringues. Very happy times were spent in these delightful little villages. After a comparatively mild winter, Spring was already peeping into the woods and fields and weaving pale primroses and deep blue violets into the earth's new carpet. Warm sunshine flooded hill and vale, and had a cheering influence. Training was carried out under happy conditions, and, after weeks of trench life with its attendant strain, physical and mental, this mild work proved a great tonic. On certain days leave was granted, when motor buses conveyed happy parties to St. Omer and to Boulogne-sur-Mer. But, alas! this restful and happy time was short-lived. Two weeks had quickly passed when news came through that the enemy had at last launched his long-expected attack. At this time one little dreamed that he was to almost succeed in sweeping through France.

So kits were packet, blankets rolled, and at dawn on the 23rd of March the Battalion left the peaceful little villages to commence a long, weary struggle of months of terrific warfare.

Lumbres was reached after an hour's march, and here the Battalion had to wait until 2 p.m. for the train which was to convey it to Caestre. Trains were everywhere rushing troops toward the line to stem the tide of grey-clad figures which had flooded over it in many places. This sudden strain upon the railways had upset their daily programmes, and no definite information regarding the train service could be given by railway officials.

Caestre was reached about 4 p.m. when a long march lay before the Battalion which had been ordered to proceed to billets in Winnizeele.

After half an hour's march along a cobblestone road the Unit turned aside into a green lane, and towards sunset halted for the evening meal, when friendly comrades-in-arms, the New Zealanders, set to work boiling water and making tea, and from their own canteen bought biscuits which they handed out to the "Aussies." In the meantime, an order arrived direct from Corps which cancelled the previous order of movement and instructed the Battalion to proceed to billets at Wallon Cappel.

The march was resumed at dusk, and hours after the stars had peeped out from a cloudless sky the long column still tramped along cobblestone roads, through villages, and out into the open country where lights twinkled from scattered farmhouses.

Packs and equipment seemed to grow heavier and heavier, and when at last billets were reached everyone was worn out after a long, hard day of eighteen hours. In large barns, where the farmers liberally supplied the travellers with straw, the Battalion settled down for the night, and soon everyone was soundly sleeping; "A" Company sharing a large barn with French refugees who had fled from Hazebrouck, which town was being heavily bombarded by the advancing enemy.

At 3 o'clock in the morning the Battalion was instructed to proceed to Wardrecques area, but this order was cancelled by later instructions, and after breakfast a move was made to a road junction slightly north of Wallon Cappel, where motor buses were to pick up the Unit.

Orders of movements were frequently altered. The successful break-through of the enemy had disorganised whole armies, and from time to time the movements of battalions were upset. The march to the place where the motor buses were to be met was by a round about way of several miles. Orders were issued that bodies of troops must not travel along certain main roads. The result was that to reach a place half a mile distant two hours' solid marching might be necessary. This was the Battalion's experience at Wallon Cappel, and was the subject of much bitter criticism.

The buses conveyed the Unit to Campagne, where it marched across from the main road into an open field, when blankets were taken from packs and stacked in readiness to be taken on to billets by the Transport Section. It was a great relief to be free to march on without blankets; one's pack, equipment and ammunition were certainly a heavy enough burden without the additional weight of blankets.

Once again the journey was continued, and after a hard march of two and a half hours, the neighborhood of Coubronne was reached, when Headquarters was established at Le Rons. "B" Company billeted at Coubronne, and "A", "C" and "D" Companies at Le Sablon.

The Battalion remained in these villages until 11.30 on the following night, March 25th. This rest of over 24 hours was badly needed.

Moving on again the March was to St. Omer railway station, which was reached at four o'clock in the morning.

A disorganised train service kept the Battalion waiting for fives hours in the vicinity of the station. It was a raw morning, and, added to this heavy rain fell just before daybreak and soaked through the thickest overcoats.

Three Companies, 'A", "B". and "D", entrained for the South at 9 a.m. "C" Company was to follow by a later train. At that time it waes not known to what place the Unit was proceeding; probably to Doullens, it was thought.

But at four o'clock in the afternoon the Battalion detrained at Mondicourt. Here the Railway Traffic Officer stated that enemy armoured cars were but three miles away. The roads were choked with an unending stream of traffic coming from the direction where the enemy was supposed to be. Refugees were fleeing with what possessions they could take with them and many a pitiful sight touched the hearts of men used to the callousness of war.

Along the dusty road an old woman would be leading her cow; a young mother fleeing with her babe and a small bundle of clothes snatched together in a few frenzied moments of terror when the news came that "the Allemand was coming"; an old lumbering dray piled up with mattresses and house furniture. a middle-aged woman with a large family of frightened children clinging to her bedraggled skirts. Along the roads, dodging in and out among motor lorries, cars and artillery waggons, these poor, homeless people turned their faces towards strange towns and villages, not knowing where their next meal was to come from or where they should rest their wearied bodies when night came.

Such scenes the Battalion witnessed on the march to Authie, and they caused men to grit their teeth and press on to meet those who were the cause of such misery.

Marching on, large bodies of retiring troops were met; many were disorganised and leaderless, and one seemed to read the word defeat in the dejected faces. An atmosphere of depression seemed to enwrap the country, and passers by flung back fragments of disquieting, but as it was afterwards discovered, wholly unreliable news. Here discipline was put to the test. Worn-out by days of marching and lack of rest the Battalion was pushing on to meet the enemy while others were retiring in disorder, and informing the Australians that they would soon be doing likewise. It seemed that they alone were to face the advancing hordes. What a temptation to turn back and join the disordered Units! What chance had a mere handful of men against the massed divisions of Germany. No doubt, such thoughts occupied the mind of every man of the Battalion. Men cursed the heat, the dust, and the heavy packs. What a relief it would be to throw the latter aside and retire. But they marched on with dogged persistence.

And yet the Australians have been dubbed an undisciplined lot! Here was the true test of discipline, perhaps the severest ever put upon men, who cursed but "carried on."

At 7 p.m. Authie was reached. The only indication of the enemy's presence was that aeroplanes were dropping bombs in the neighborhood.

By eight o'clock the Battalion was settled down in billets, and, after a drink of hot tea everyone (with the exception of the scouts who were scouring the neighborhood for any signs of the enemy) crept into their blankets.

Scarcely it seemed, had one fallen asleep when the order came to "stand to" ready for pushing on again. This was at 2 a.m., and after a scratch breakfast had been swallowed by those lucky enough to get it, the march to Marieum was commenced.

Arriving at this place at 5 a.m., the Battalion embussed for Franvillers, which was reached at 1.30 p.m.

IX.—GIBRALTAR: A TYPICAL PILL BOX.

XI.—GROUP OF 38th BATTALION OFFICERS, ALDERSHOT CAMP, NEUVE EGLISE, JANUARY, 1918.

XII.—GROUP OF 38th BATTALION N.C.O.'S, ALDERSHOT CAMP, NEUVE EGLISE, JANUARY, 1918.

CHAPTER V.

STEMMING THE GERMAN TIDE.

Forming up in a field, orders were awaited for the next move. Half a mile away enemy shells were raising clouds of dust. Ordered to push on to Heilly the Unit immediately proceeded to that town by platoons at 200 yards intervals. Here it was reported that the enemy had reached the vicinity. Moving forward in open order the Battalion crossed the green fields lying between Heilly and Mericourt l'Abbe. At the latter place previously selected positions were taken over from the 43rd Battalion A.I.F.

There was no sign of the enemy, and by nightfall "A" and "B" Companies had established a defence line beyond Mericourt l'Abbe railway station, "C" Company being in support and "D" Company in reserve.

At 8 a.m. on the following morning, March 28th, Captain F. E. Fairweather, M.C., pushed forward with "C" Company and occupied Marrett Wood, about 1000 yards beyond the main line of defence. From there the enemy was observed in force upon a distant ridge, and his machine guns played upon the positions taken up in the wood without doing any harm.

Shortly afterwards he advanced down the side of a hill in four waves, about 100 strong, and moved towards the wood evidently bent upon capturing it.

But the attack was quickly beaten back by rifle and Lewis Gun fire, the enemy suffering 50 per cent. casualties.

The survivors retired as quickly as possible over the hill. After this futile attack the day remained comparatively quiet (except that artillery fire increased) when the positions in the wood were consolidated as much as possible. The only artillery support was one battery of eighteen pounders, which on account of the activities of its gunners, must have caused the Boche to think that there were several batteries around Mericourt. Into this town he poured a number of heavy shells, and shelled the neighborhood at random.

The night of the 28th March passed very quietly, except for occasional machine gun and artillery fire. The Battalion's casualties for 24 hours, from noon of the 28th to noon on the 29th, were two N.C.O.'s and nine other ranks wounded.

Strict watch was kept upon the hills and ridges scarcely a mile beyond the lines of defence. At any moment a sea of grey figures might swarm down them, and rush the positions held by mere handfuls of men. If it succeeded in breaking through there was nothing to block its onward rush to Amiens, for there were no troops in support of the several Australian Brigades defending a wide front.

Early in the morning of the 29th a patrol of two N.C.O.'s and fourteen men, under Lieut. G. E. Fitzgerald, moved out to reconnoitre a hill in front of Marrett Wood (near Treux), "C" Company's position, to find out whether it was occupied by the enemy. Very soon a party of Boche, about 40 strong, was surprised in a sunken road a few hundred yards out from the wood. This party was immediately engaged by oblique Lewis

Gun and rifle fire from a few yards range, and in a minute or two was mown down. About forty casualties were inflicted, and three prisoners were secured by the patrol. No further signs of the enemy's whereabouts could be discovered.

Between the occasional disturbances caused by enemy shells a brooding silence seemed to settle over the woods and hills. These were disquieting days. Just where the enemy would launch his next attack no one could say. In what strength he might be massing behind the near skyline no one could venture to surmise.

On the 30th March, four days after arriving at Mericourt. "A" Company took over Marrett Wood from "C" Company, the latter retiring to the village for a few hours' rest. This change over took place about mid-day. Scarcely had "A" Company entered the wood when enemy shells crashed into it, heavy shrapnel being frequently used. Two officers, two N.C.O.'s and five men were wounded, and Pte. Marion was killed. During its occupation of the wood, "A" Company had an exceptionally rough time, having to bear the brunt of the enemy's shelling.

The next move by the Boche took place on the following day, when the 11th Brigade, on the right, was attacked. Wave after wave of German Infantry swept onward, but the assault was heavily repulsed, and the attacking troops collapsed under the withering fire of machine guns and rifles.

The fearful punishment which all attacking parties received on this front must have broken the confident spirit of the enemy, and he, no doubt, began to realise that his advance was being effectively checked.

By this time spirits had been raised by the roaring of the 3rd Division artillery which had hastened to the assistance of the infantry. Batteries, from eighteen pounders upwards, now barked viciously and poured their salvos of screaming shells into the enemy territory.

Our aeroplanes and those of the enemy were now actively searching for batteries and troops with the result that many thrilling battles were fought in mid-air.

On the last day of March the Unit relieved the 39th Battalion in forward positions, when trenches hastily dug a few days before were put in better condition. Weather conditions since arriving in this sector were far from being good. Heavy rains fell from time to time, and men were wet through for the trenches, as yet, afforded no protection from the weather.

By the 2nd April enemy artillery and machine gun fire had increased, but the movements of enemy troops had decreased. Evidently he had got into fixed positions and secured some shelter. The Battalion's snipers were kept busy, for the enemy would often show himself, jumping from post to post. Many hits were claimed by the snippers, and scouts brought in an enemy machine gun and also many documents and other spoil. On the 3rd April there was a marked increase in all activities of the enemy. Near Morlancourt he was using seven observation balloons. At night he was now using Verey lights and night flares, and was putting up wire.

The Battalion sector was now greatly improved. Outposts were nearly all connected and some wire entanglements were constructed, and the digging of a communication trench was commenced.

On the night of April 3rd the Unit was relieved by the 40th Battalion, the relief being accomplished systematically and without interference by the enemy. The Battalion retired to Ribemont, about a mile and a half from Mericourt, when it became known as "D" Battalion.

On the following afternoon a warning by wire was received from Brigade Headquarters of the possibility of an enemy attack. German prisoners captured stated that their troops were already in position for the event, so our artillery opened up on his posts and probable points of assembly, and for three hours maintained a heavy fire. The night passed quietly and at 5 a.m. all our artillery fired rapidly on enemy posts and possible places of formation. At 7 a.m., enemy heavy guns commenced counter battery work in an attempt to neutralise our field guns east of the village. A great deal of shelling ensued, but our guns remained in action throughout the artillery battle. Gas shells were frequently used by the enemy, but only a faint trace of gas reached Ribemont.

At 7.50 the shelling lifted to the village and the cross roads. The vicinity of "C" and "D" Companies billets and Headquarters was heavily bombarded for 60 minutes. Only slight casualties occurred, for troops took to cellars and dispersed over the fields.

At 8.50 the bombardment lifted west toward Heilly, but intermittent shelling of Ribemont continued all day. Everyone was retained at billets as the enemy was attacking the front line, but as he was beaten off no movement was necessary on the part of the Battalion. While in reserve working parties were almost daily employed digging strong posts in the neighborhood in case the Boche should break through. Owing to enemy observation training could not be carried out, but the Scout Officer organised the scouts and gave lectures on their work, under new and unusual conditions of semi-open warfare; and the Signalling-Officer organised signallers for the next relief of the trenches.

On the night of 6th April the Battalion took over the trenches in the Buire-Treux sector. The relief was carried out without enemy interruption during heavy rain. On the following day Buire village was shelled, but its garrison was housed in cellars and no casualties occurred.

The Acting C.O. (Major Hurry) spent the day in the front line viewing the dispositions, which it was decided, were not the best possible, and a scheme for their improvement was submitted to higher authority. This scheme was immediately approved and steps were taken to commence the wiring and digging of new posts.

On the eighth day of the month the troops were fully occupied in improving defences and endeavoring to obtain a little comfort and shelter from the inclement weather. Enemy artillery was still very active. The Battalion snipers and Lewis Gunners were kept busy although there was not much enemy movement. Observers drew the attention of the artillery upon a party of the enemy which was observed. The artillery shot accurately and the party, 90 strong, dispersed from huts in which it had been encamped.

When night came the 38th Battalion advanced a portion of the line on a front of 700 yards, constructed new posts, and placed out wire; this was done by "A" and "B" Companies. The scouts of "B" Company executed a daring patrol to a distant objective and obtained close touch with the enemy and brought back documents and Verey lights from enemy dead.

Next day the enemy harassed the area with shell fire. Between the hours of 8.30 and 9.30 a.m. he distributed over a thousand shells on Buire and Treux villages, and on the railway line held by the Battalion. Owing to a misty atmosphere the day was favorable for an enemy attack, and the shelling seemed to indicate this intention; but the enemy infantry remained inactive and the shelling continued all day, varying considerably in violence.

At 9 p.m. the Unit was relieved by the 40th Battalion when it moved back to Mericourt and occupied support trenches and became known as "C" Battalion. Battalion Headquarters was established in a chateau in Artillery Row, Mericourt.

Although rations as usually issued were on a somewhat limited scale and lacked variety, the conditions of their issue reflected very creditably on the work of the Quartermaster (Lieut. P. J. Telfer) and his staff, and also on that of the Transport Section. Rations were cooked and prepared at the Quartermaster's Store at Heilly. The vessels containing the food were then packed in straw-filled boxes and carried on limbers to the front line area, being issued to the troops in pleasant variety and satisfying quantity; two hot meals being given, one before daylight, and one after dusk, as transport was impossible during daylight.

Trench feet had been prevented by the daily exchange of soiled, wet socks for clean dry ones. Although no laundries had been instituted in this as yet, unorganised front the Quartermaster had secured by salvage and other means a surplus of socks which were washed and dried at the store and issued daily in exchange for soiled pairs.

The activities of March 11th were those of artillery and aircraft on both sides. Four enemy balloons were observing from the vicinity of Morlancourt. Defences had been further improved by wiring and entrenchments, and the area was rapidly becoming organised in depth.

On April 12th the Battalion relieved the 40th Battalion astride the River Ancre. "A" and "B" Companies occupied the front line left of the river, and "D" Company was on the right bank and parallel with it to a post astride the Buire-Ville-sur-Ancre road. "C" Company was in reserve in Buire, and Headquarters was established in an old farm house in a wood, known as the Haunted House.

At 4 o'clock on the morning of the 14th, "A" Company's patrol of six men encountered an enemy patrol, eight strong, near a disabled tank 400yds east of the line. The enemy threw two grenades, which slightly wounded four men, and then scattered, apparently escaping the rifle fire of "A" Company's patrol.

The front was now firmly established and while it was quite possible that the enemy might make an attempt to break through, everyone was confident that it would be beaten back and prove a disastrous business to the Boche. His artillery was continually active, and at intervals shells were poured into the villages of Buire and Treux.

It was in the front line about 100 yards out from the latter village that a very popular officer of the Battalion (Lieut. T. H. Kennedy, M.C.) was killed by a shell on the 15th April.

On being relieved once again the Unit retired to Ribemont. During the four days in the line 350 yards of new wire was put up and 250 yards of existing wire was strengthened; 280 yards of new trench was dug.

The next five days were busy ones when much work was done on rear defences.

The days which followed until the Battalion moved back to rest billets in Allonville were strenuous ones. The Unit had two more trips into the line. Every day and night the enemy bombarded the villages now slowly, but surely, becoming mere heaps of ruins.

But only with his artillery did the Boche succeed, for his troops were never to set foot upon the soil held against such great odds in those first weeks when his advance was effectively checked.

When at last the sector was taken over by the 21st Battalion A.I.F., on 9th May, it was a body of tired, nerve-racked men that retired to the peace and quietude of the delightful little town of Allonville.

Here it seemed Spring had prepared a welcome for all, for the village gardens and the surrounding fields and woods were a source of delight.

The hours of morning were spent in mild training and the afternoon was devoted to recreation. Delightful walks through the flower-filled grounds of a large chateau, and quiet hours spent in the adjacent woods or open fields, proved a wonderful pick-me-up, and within a few days the strained look was missing from the faces of those who had been tested almost to breaking point.

On Sunday morning, 12th May, Church Parade was held in the chateau grounds where the songbirds added their voices to the singing of hymns.

After the parade there was a presentation of medals by General Sir Wm. Birdwood.

On Tuesday, 12th, the 10th Brigade was inspected by the Commander-in-Chief, Sir Douglas Haig.

The day was warm and sunny and the Brigade's turnout reflected great credit upon it. At the conclusion of the inspection Sir Douglas thanked the Brigade for the wonderful work it had done in helping to check the enemy's advance.

On the 18th May a Brigade Transport Competition was held, with specially-selected judges from Divisional Staff. The 38th Battalion Transport Section won first prize for all events, which consisted of:—

(1) Complete Section turnout.

(2) Best pair of heavy draught horses and cooker. (Driver A. H. Shapland).

(3) Best pair light draught horses and waggon. (Driver S. McCorkell).

(4) Best pair mules and waggon. (Driver H. R. Box).

The judgment was based on the general turnout as to appearances, care bestowed, and grooming of animals, etc., no points being given for type or particular excellence of animals, and to win under these conditions reflected the greatest credit on the general work of the section.

Several eagerly-contested football matches were held during the stay at Allonville and drew large crowds of enthusiastic supporters.

About three miles across the fields lay the City of Amiens, where the world-famed cathedral towered above the city's buildings. Enemy shells occasionally crashed into the old town, now deserted by its inhabitants. Amiens attracted enemy night-bombing 'planes which on two occasions passed over Allonville to receive a warm reception from the Battalion's anti-aircraft Lewis Gunners. On the second visit of the aeroplanes a big Gotha, finding Allonville district too warm a place, turned and fled after dropping his load of bombs in the Chateau grounds. Unfortunately one bomb fell near the 10th Field Ambulance, killing a corporal and wounding others.

After two weeks' rest at Allonville the Battalion moved up to a reserve area in the vicinity of Blangy Tronville to take over from a battalion of the 4th Division. The march was a fairly stiff one, for the day was inclined to be hot, and the roads were very dusty. Towards the end of the journey it was seen that this new area should prove a very pleasant place, for the Somme Canal, with its clear running water, promised good bathing. By midday the four Companies of the Battalion bivouaced in the vicinity of the railway line.

Headquarters was at the cross roads a few hundred yards distant; rear B.H.Q. being at Blangy Tronville.

After everyone had settled down in dugouts and had a refreshing meal, the canal was visited and here in the clear water running between an avenue of shady trees, a delightful afternoon was spent; swimming, diving and pulling about in old punts.

On 24th May, Lieut.-Colonel C. H. Davis, D.S.O., was promoted Colonel to command the A.I.F. Base at Le Havre. Major G. Hurry, D.S.O., Acting O.C. of the Battalion, was promoted temporary Lieut.-Colonel to command the Unit. Lieut.-Colonel Hurry was an extremely popular officer; a clear-headed, fearless man who was always keenly interested in the welfare of every individual member of the Battalion.

It was with mingled feeling of regret and happiness that the Battalion said farewell to Colonel Davis—regret because it was losing its C.O., the C.O. who had guided and led it through the most arduous period of the Battalion's existence, and happiness because, though it realised that he was leaving, his departure meant the assumption of duties which would give greater scope to his brilliant organising ability.

All ranks had long since learned to appreciate the value of the fine pioneering work achieved by Colonel Davis. The work of organising the training and of equipping the Battalion for war had all been carried out by him, with the result that on landing in France the Battalion presented as perfect a piece of fighting mechanism as could be found in the British Army. The care, indefatigable energy and solid hard work—both physical and mental—required to discipline and train a mob of eager but untrained, undisciplined, unmilitary men for the serious business of war, is alone known to those few, comparatively, who have had that onerous duty thrown upon their shoulders.

During the period of training—often necessarily irksome and trying—one was apt to limit his perspective and wonder why certain things, to the lay mind (i.e. the mind of the trainee) obviously unnecessary—should be ordered by the C.O. But he knew. He could see further than the Battalion, and it was not long before the Unit profited by the precepts and teaching of Colonl Davis. And the long months of weary trench warfare, the merciless trench raids so often carried out by the men of the 38th; the brilliant operations at Messines; the nightmare of Passchendaele; the strenuous and nerve-racking experiences at Warneton and elsewhere, and then the rapid transition to the Somme campaign—all of which were performed under Colonel Davis—had taught all ranks what they owed to one who might justly claim the title of "Father of the Battalion."

But his successor—Major Hurry, as he then was—was a worthy heir in every respect to the legacy left him by Colonel Davis, and had the Battalion been asked to choose its new C.O. the selection would undoubtedly have fallen upon Major Hurry.

The stay in the neighborhood of Blangy Tronville was not altogether a time of rest, for the enemy strafed the area from time to time with high explosive and shrapnel, when "A" and "B" companies were often compelled to leave their dugouts and disperse in the open fields.

Working parties were supplied for cable-burying in the forward area, and members of the Battalion will have lively recollections of the nights spent in the neighborhood of Abbe Wood. The work was constantly interrupted by the enemy, who poured salvos of shells, high explosive and gas, into the field across which the cable was being laid.

At 9.30 on the night of 27th May the Unit moved by platoons at 300 yards intervals to Pioneer Switch and occupied a trench in that vicinity. This was done on instructions from high authority in order to support the 9th Brigade A.I.F. in case of an attack by the enemy which was daily expected on this front. While marching up to take up positions for the night the roads were heavily bombarded with gas shells when the Battalion had a lively passage. The night passed quietly, and at 6 a.m. the Unit moved back to Blangy Tronville.

The Battalion Echelon was situated in a wood near the village of Lamotte. While a battalion is in the vicinity of the line a certain percentage of all ranks remains in a back area. The reason for this is in case a Unit should, by the misfortune of war, be annihilated, there still remain members of that Unit upon which to build up another strong body.

On the fourth day of June the Unit relieved the 42nd Battalion in the front line of Villers-Bretonneux. The relief was completed at 1 a.m., and was without incident except that three casualties were sustained.

Villers-Bretonneux! What a medley of thoughts the name of this town conjures up in the minds of those who have lived among its ruins. Shattered houses whose tottering walls often fell to pile heaps of mortar and bricks upon the roofs of cellars, thus making them safer places of habitation. shattered houses, and yet upon their broken walls clung photographs of the members of families who once resided there in peace and happiness; furniture—cheap or expensive—in this house undamaged, in the next smashed to matchwood; rooms littered with clothing, dainty feminine wear which seemed to have no place amid such scenes of devastation and brutality.

Happy homes wrecked beyond repair by devilish shells. Verey lights going up in the night, and gaunt, distorted buildings silhouetted against their radiance. Bullets peppering the walls; night bombers droning overhead; the crashing of bombs and shells.

Villers-Bretonneux! occupied for one day only by the Boche. if you excepted his dead still lying in several of the cellars.

Here for eight days "C" and "D" Companies occupied the front line just beyond the town, and "A" and "B" Companies the support trenches connecting up with cellars.

Enemy artillery and machine guns were very active and the trenches and town were from time to time subjected to heavy bombardments. Working parties engaged in digging trenches linking up outposts were continually interrupted by enemy fire. A small orchard seemed to be a centre of considerable enemy activity, there being at least three light machine guns in its vicinity. During the night of 11th June the enemy searched the whole of the forward area with one or two guns. Probably the working parties had disturbed him, and he feared an attack.

These days in the line were, indeed, trying ones; days of uncertainty, when death lurked among the ruins of the houses, and walked through the trenches.

In the support line, occupied by "A" Company, several of the old boys of the Battalion laid down their lives and their comrades quietly carried them away for their long rest.

HISTORY OF 38th BATTALION, A.I.F.

The Battalion was relieved on the 12th June, "B" Company remaining in Villers-Bretonneux for special work under the control of the 40th Battalion, and the remaining companies moving back about a mile and a half to points on the railway line; Battalion Headquarters was established at the monastry in Bois l'Abbe.

During the next six days working parties were employed in the forward and reserve areas, the main work being done in the front line.

The trenches were again taken over on 18th June. This second time of occupation of the line passed in much the same way as had the previous.

The Orchard still remained a centre for enemy activity, although rifle grenades were proving very effective in silencing the machine guns. Enemy artillery was fairly active. On the night of 20th June it was estimated that over 300 shells fell in the forward area.

Four officers and ten other ranks of the American forces were attached to the Companies for several days to gain experience in line work.

On 23rd June the Battalion was relieved and retired to the neighborhood of Blangy Tronville, and three days later moved back to bivouacs in a wood near Allonville which was reached just before nightfall. On the following day companies were thoroughly overhauled in matters appertaining to clothing and equipment when damaged or lost articles were replaced.

Next morning, 28th June, a move was made to bivouac on an embankment on the Hallue River, just beyond the town of Querrieu.

This new camp proved a most delightful spot. Just below the embankment with its snug little dugouts lay the river, and, here and there, fine swimming pools gleamed invitingly among acres of green rushes. The surrounding fields were ablaze with scarlet poppies, and warm sunshine flooded the land.

Not for long after the arrival of the Battalion did the swimming pools retain their calm surfaces, for after a hot, dusty march everybody made for the water.

Happy days followed. Training of a mild nature was carried out in the mornings, but in the afternoon all were free to spend the hours as they pleased. Cricket matches were held, and one whole day was devoted to a Battalion sports meeting, when prize money was donated from Regimental funds. This day was a most enjoyable one. The sports were held on a green flat which proved an ideal running ground. The weather was pleasantly warm and a neighboring swimming pool proved a side attraction in between the events. On one night the peace and quietness of the camp at the river's edge was rudely disturbed when enemy 'planes heavily bombed the vicinity. For several disquieting minutes the big Gothas hovered over the river and bombs crashed among the trees, their explosions shaking the dugouts along the embankment as volcanoes of flame leaped up from the ground. Happily no one was injured, and on the 'planes passing on to another area the camp was soon wrapped in sleep.

On the evening of 8th July a "stand-to" was ordered by Army Headquarters. Immediately all was rush and bustle. "Marching Order" had to be fitted together and valises packed. The Battalion was in battle position by 9.18 p.m.—the first battalion of the Division to be in position.

The Unit regretfully bade farewell to the Hallue River on 11th July, and marched to bivouacs, which were taken over from the 14th Battalion A.I.F. Resting until dusk and then moving on in accordance with orders to a forward area, the Unit passed through the town of Corbie about eleven o'clock to occupy reserve trenches about two miles beyond the town. These trenches (which lay among wheat fields) were in very good order, having good dugouts. Here a stay of six days was made. During that time the area was subjected to a great deal of shelling, and anti-aircraft gunners were kept busy by enemy 'planes.

On the night of 17th July the Battalion took over the front line and supports from the 39th Battalion beyond Vaire Wood on the right of the village of Hammel from whence the Boche had been driven back a fortnight previously by American and Australian troops.

The line was taken over under adverse conditions as a Brigade on the right was also "taking over" a portion of enemy territory to straighten the line. The natural result was that the enemy strafed all along the line, fearing a general attack. Unfortunately a number of "D" Company became casualties while moving up through Vaire Wood. Upon the occupation of the trenches the scouts immediately made a reconnaisance of the line to decide upon the positions for outposts, and incidentally discovered an enemy post in a German communication trench near Accroche Street. The accommodation in the trenches was found to be inadequate, necessitating night working parties. Every night, parties were engaged digging new trenches and outposts, and protecting them by the erection of barbed wire entanglements. Some very lively times were experienced while on this work out in No Man's Land, and when back in the comparative safety of the trenches. The enemy strafed the defences from time to time with high explosive and high velocity shells of a small calibre, commonly known as "whizz-bangs."

The latter shells had a nasty knack of skimming (so it seemed) just above the parapets, and their sudden swish! swish! swish! would quickly cause one to duck down well below ground level.

A story is told in "Aussie," the Australian soldiers' magazine, of two "Diggers" who were sent scurrying off to their dugouts by a shower of "whizzbangs."

When in the seclusion of a strong dugout one said to the other: "Did you hear that first one?" "Did I hear it? Cripes! I heard it twice. I heard it as it passed ME, and I heard it again as I passed IT on my way to this funkhole."

Battalion Headquarters, which was situated in a donga below Central Copse (behind Vaire Wood) also received its share of "whizzbangs."

The weather was mild, but thunderstorms were constantly brewing, and heavy downpours of rain caused inconvenience and discomfort in the trenches.

The moon was approaching the full and was likely to outline parties working nightly out in No Man's Land. At 1.30 on the morning of the 19th Captain Selleck, O.C. "C" Company, was shot by a sniper while visiting an outpost. His death was a great loss to the Battalion, for he was a most capable officer.

On one occasion "A" Company had a rather disconcerting time, being strafed from the front and rear. This was due to our artillery and machine guns firing low.

The Unit was relieved on 25th July, when it retired to a gully behind Vaire Wood.

If you climbed the surrounding slopes, risking odd shells and an occasional sprinkle of machine gun bullets, a fine view could be had of the country stretching away to Amiens. The fields were everywhere gay with summer flowers. Patches of scarlet poppies and blue seas of cornflowers colored the land. About two miles away the massive twin towers of Corbie Cathedral rose above the town and its surrounding woods. The Somme wound its silvered way among the woods and hills, and far away in the west the stately spire of Amiens Cathedral gleamed like a needle. No doubt the enemy watchers beholding the spires and domes of that coveted city must have realised that their wild dream of conquest was losing its rosy hues and was slowly fading. Everywhere along the line his attacks had been repulsed, when his losses had been enormous.

Soon the Allied armies were to sweep down upon him and steadily press him back to, and beyond, that line from where in March he had swept onward to all appearances victorious.

Already there were rumors of a big push in the near future, and by the time the Battalion again occupied the trenches beyond Vaire Wood, special parties were reconnoitring the area, and on still nights the rumbling and clattering of tanks could be heard as they trundled along to take up secluded positions where they could not be observed by the enemy. By 5th August troops were thickening up behind the line, so the day of the attack could not be far away.

At last word came through that the great event so carefully planned would take place in the early hours of Thursday, 8th August, to be known as "Z" day, and that the 10th Brigade would form the support brigade of the 3rd Division, which was attacking on this front. A few hours before the attack the troops holding the front line were withdrawn to positions behind Vaire Wood, and their places were taken by attacking troops, 33rd and 34th Battalions A.I.F.

CHAPTER VI.

THE GREAT OFFENSIVE, AND THE BATTLE OF PROYART.

A thick mist making conditions for attack favorable enshrouded the land when the first glimmer of dawn cast a faint light over the area. Zero hour had been fixed for 4.20 a.m. when as one gun the artillery for miles along the line opened out upon the enemy.

Never will that moment be forgotten. The sudden roar from thousands of steel throats; the swish! swish! swish! of thousands of shells rushing down upon the Boche followed by the "drumfire" of the guns, whose crews, bared to the waist, toiled to feed the ravenous breeches. Every now and then the heavy booming of big naval guns back in the woods near Corbie, rose above the staccato notes of the eighteen pounders and howitzers. The lumbering tanks moved out from their places of hiding and waddled across the trenches to lead the Infantry.

Imagine the enemy's terror when suddenly awakened by that tornado of shells mercilessly smashing his defences, and then, when the barrage lifted back, to behold the tanks looming up through the mist like the monsters of a nightmare, crushing everything in their way to matchwood, and spitting death from their iron loopholes through which were thrust the muzzles of machine guns, and between and behind the tanks the infantry, cool and determined, advancing with fixed bayonets. That was quite enough for the Boche; rifles were thrown down, equipment stripped off, and up went their hands, and with lusty cries of "Kamarad.," they tried to make themselves heard above the clattering of the tanks. On went the tanks and infantry, and the Boche passed nervously through them, prisoners to make their way to the rear, where they were collected in groups and marched away to the Prisoners of War cages.

Fritz had been caught napping. Even his gunners were were asleep in dugouts when our artillery opened out. The result was that several minutes elapsed ere his guns opened out in a feeble reply. Aeroplanes had marked the positions of many of his batteries, the majority of which were quickly silenced by our gunners. Old machine gun posts in rear put up a half-hearted resistance, but these were quickly put out of action by the tanks and the infantry that passed on practically without opposition.

News of their success soon came back. Accroche Wood, Tailloux Wood, and other enemy strong points had been taken. An advance of a thousand yards had been made, and they were steadily pressing on and were likely to drive the enemy back for a distance of six or seven miles. Overhead aeroplanes were watching their progress, swooping down out of the mist every now and then like giant bats, and dropping ammunition and rations if required. Occasionally a German 'plane would be observed, to be quickly driven off or brought to earth by the guardians in the air. And in the neighborhood of Vaire Wood where the 38th Battalion awaited the word to push on, men now walked about in the open in those places where a few hours previously enemy shells had crashed from time to time and the sibilant hiss of bullets had been heard.

When you have lived for days in trenches continually subjected to shell fire it is with a strange feeling that you climb out of those trenches and walk with absolute safety along their parapets. Somehow or other they don't seem to be the same trenches. Here is the little "bivvie" in which you crouched last night when "whizzbangs" made you hold your breath for a few long moments. Now you sit on the parapet above it, and smoke a cigarette. Yesterday had you been offered six months "Blighty leave" to sit there for 30 seconds you wouldn't have taken the risk. Last night there was an air of mystery lurking in No Man's Land. Perhaps a few nights ago you cautiously crawled out into it with the scouts while bullets hissed in the grass at your side. Now you calmly stroll over this area where gay poppies nod saucily in the sunshine. Somehow or other you didn't expect to find flowers blooming here. Yesterday flowers would have seemed out of place in No Man's Land. But they were there all the time, calmly lifting their faces to the sky. At 4.30 p.m. the Battalion commanded by Major A. J. A. Maudsley pushed on to Hamilton Valley.

Although the move forward was a rather tiring affair (for the afternoon was warm, and everyone was loaded up with gear and ammunition) it was, perhaps, the most interesting march the Battalion had had for many a long day. Naturally, all were curious to see the effect of the morning barrage. That the Boch had been caught napping was soon seen, for in a gully several of the enemy dead were found in a state of undress. Those behind his line who had fled before the attack had left most of their personal belongings behind them in their haste to get away from the tanks and the infantry. Crossing the fields all sorts of odds and ends were picked up, one man finding an Iron Cross carefully wrapped up in tissue paper.

Several of our tanks had been put out of order by enemy shells and were stranded in the fields, and squatting there is frog-like attitudes.

Far away over the eastern horizon an enemy balloon was peeping up and evidently directing a high velocity gun which occasionally sent over a nine inch shell to raise a cloud of dust and smoke in the wheat crops traversed by the Battalion.

The dawn of August 9th found the Unit fairly comfortably bivouaced in Hamilton Valley. How all ranks appreciated the freedom from the restraints of trench warfare! Lieut.-Colonel Hurry was missing the consummation of his, as well as every members', desire, that of getting Fritz well and truly in the open. The Colonel. owing to sickness, had left the Battalion, bitterly disappointed at the trick Fate had played him. Knowing his thoughts were with them, all hoped to play up to his fighting standard.

After holding the trench line facing Accroche Wood for six weeks this move into enemy territory had wonderfully revived the spirits of all.

The 10th A.I.F. Brigade during the ensuing operations was to come directly under the orders of the 4th Divisional Commander acting as his reserve Brigade.

Early on the morning of the 9th, instructions reached Battalion Headquarters that an officer from Headquarters and each Company must push forward and reconnoitre the left of the established line held by the 16th Battalion A.I.F. from the Somme, west of Mericourt-sur-Somme. This was satisfactorily accomplished, but unfortunately the Battalion's possible position was altered to the right half of the line, held by 14th Battalion, necessitating another move forward, the outpost line being approximately 4500 yards from Hamilton Valley. No wonder those doing both trips slept well, although before retiring to their several "funk holes", descriptions of the 9th Brigade and Americans' attack north of the river, for the purpose of clearing the village of Chipilly and establishing in front of Etinehem Wood, was freely discussed. Those out with the 14th Battalion had a grand view of the combination of tanks and infantry in attack, and saw what grand assistance is a shrapnel barrage put down by eighteen pounders.

Unfortunately, various "Diggers" of the 38th Battalion pushed forward from Hamilton Valley to view this attack, and from the 14th Battalion outposts were plainly visible to the naked eye, the result being that Fritz opened upon them with a high velocity battery, and sent them scurrying back to the shelter of the valley.

Although the nights were sharp, the days were bright and warm, that of 10th August being similar to the Australian early Autumn.

The result of the reconnaissance showed the enemy to be holding in considerable force a line running from Etinehem through Mericourt-sur-Somme, bending south-east towards Framerville and Vauvillers.

About 10 a.m. the Acting C.O. was called to a conference at Brigade Headquarters, situated at the south end of Hamilton Valley. At 2 p.m. the C.O. called together Company Commanders and explained the operation projected. The intention was that the Brigade, accompanied by six tanks and an attached Light Trench Mortar Battery and machine guns, was to make a night march along the main Warfusee Road into enemy territory as far as Avenue Cross, and then turn north following the road line to Chuignolles, junctioning with the 9th Brigade that was making a night attack through Etinehem to secure the spur running south to the Somme.

Night signals were arranged, two white lights in quick succession when established on the anticipated line to be answered by the northern force when also established. Unfortunately, these were never fired by the 10th Brigade. The object was to cut off a known large enemy occupation together with a valuable enemy dump known as La Flaque dump.

The 37th Battalion was to be on the left of the projected line; on their right, 38th Battalion; while on their right again was to be the 40th Battalion; the 39th Battalion to be in the front line as support.

At 5 o'clock on the morning of the 11th an advance was to be made from the front line, and the enemy force was to be sandwiched between this and the projected line to be held by the 10th Brigade.

Simultaneously the 6th Brigade was to push forward through Framerville and Rainecourt, linking up on the right of the 10th Brigade. Great assistance was to be expected from the artillery, the task of the heavies being Chuignes and the steep valley running south-west from that village, as a concentration of Boche artillery had been located there. The only reconnissance for this operation was that from aeroplane reports and armoured cars that had made a dash out from Harbonnieres through Framerville and back.

The portion of the projected line to be held by the 38th Battalion was practically parallel with the road running from Chuignolles to Framerville, extending from the corner of Robin Wood to a little distance south, the 40th Battalion continuing the line to Avenue Cross.

※ ※ ※ ※

PROYART.

38th BATTALION.

C.O., Major A. J. A. Maudsley, his H.Q. Staff and Company Officers.

HEADQUARTERS.

Adjutant, Captain A. Fraser, M.C.
R.M.O., Captain G. V. Davis, D.S.O.
I. O. and Liason Officer, Lieut. C. T. Crispe
L. G. O. and Scout Officer, Lieut. G. A. Dutton.
Sig. Officer, Lieut. E. Potter.
Transport Officer, Lieut. F. B. Langley.
Quartermaster, Acting Lieut. H. R. Robbins.

"A" COMPANY.
Capt. F. E. Fairweather, M.C.
Lieut. C. H. Peters, M.C.
Lieut. D. McG. Addison.
Lieut. E. J. H. Schlitz, M.C.

"B" COMPANY.
Capt. L. J. Beattie.
Lieut. W. F. Bennett.
Lieut. N. W. Sandiford.
Lieut. S. R. Warnock.

"C" COMPANY.
Capt. H. Dench.
Lieut. H. McColl.
Lieut. E. M. Barker.
Lieut. F. J. Baxter.

"D" COMPANY.
Capt. W. H. Orchard, M.C.
Lieut. H. F. Poole.
Lieut. R. B. Riddell.
Lieut. J. C. Davis.

The Battalion moved from Hamilton Valley at 6.30 p.m., working forward in artillery formation led by Headquarters Company, followed by "A" Company (O.C., Capt. F. E. Fairweather, M.C.). "B" Company (Capt. L. J. Beattie); "C" Company (Captain H. Dench); "D" Company (Capt. W. H. Orchard, M.C.), the starting point being the road junction where the tanks were to join up. It was intended that the head of the column pass the starting point at 9.30 p.m., but owing to the long twilight the hour was postponed until 10.30. The order of the movement was three tanks, accompanied by Battalion scouts at the head of the 37th Battalion, which was in the van. The 38th Battalion followed by 40th Battalion, also accompanied by three tanks with 39th Battalion in rear. The tanks, owing to the darkness, could not venture from the main road, so clancked along at the head of the column at the head of each half brigade.

How many times during the night of the 10th curses were flung in their direction it would be difficult to enumerate. The 38th Battalion passed the starting point at approximately 10.45 p.m. It was a beautiful starlight night, peaceful but dark, and hardly such as would stimulate a murderous operation, though later the hurricane bombardment which descended was sufficient to whip up even the most sluggish.

The tanks at the head of the 37th Battalion could be heard rumbling along, advertising the approach through No Man's Land.

Trouble commenced on reaching La Flaque dump, in enemy territory; machine guns firing in the direction of the tanks sounds. The Battalion was protected on both flanks by flank guards. Lieut. Baxter commanding the right, and the Scout Sgt. Cpl. Stanbury the left, a group of Battalion scouts—moving under Lieut. Dutton at the head of "B" Company in the main column—to come into operation when established on the projected line.

The enemy machine gun fire increased in intensity as the column gradually "concertinaed" forward.

On crossing the La Flaque cross roads the enemy shut down on the column a barrage. It was hell let loose. Luckily there were ditches along the roadside affording a fair amount of protection from the hail of assorted projectiles which tore down upon the road with the fury of a thousand devils. So heavy was the fire that the column, after reaching a point approximately 500 yards short of Avenue Cross, was held up, again seeking cover in the roadside ditches, while the tanks, in an aimless manner, slowly trundled from place to place, swept by showers of bullets irradiating their steel sides like swarms of fireflies. To add to the column's distress low-flying Hun 'planes were bombing and machine gunning, during which additional enemy attention the Light Trench Mortar Battery section attached to the Battalion lost limber, team and ammuniion.

Towards midnight the enemy's furious blast subsided, although the tanks, utterly useless in the dark, were still attracting machine gun fire. Word came down the column to the effect that the leading Company of the 37th Battalion had been decimated and that the Unit's Commanding Officer, Lieut.-Col. Knox-Knight,

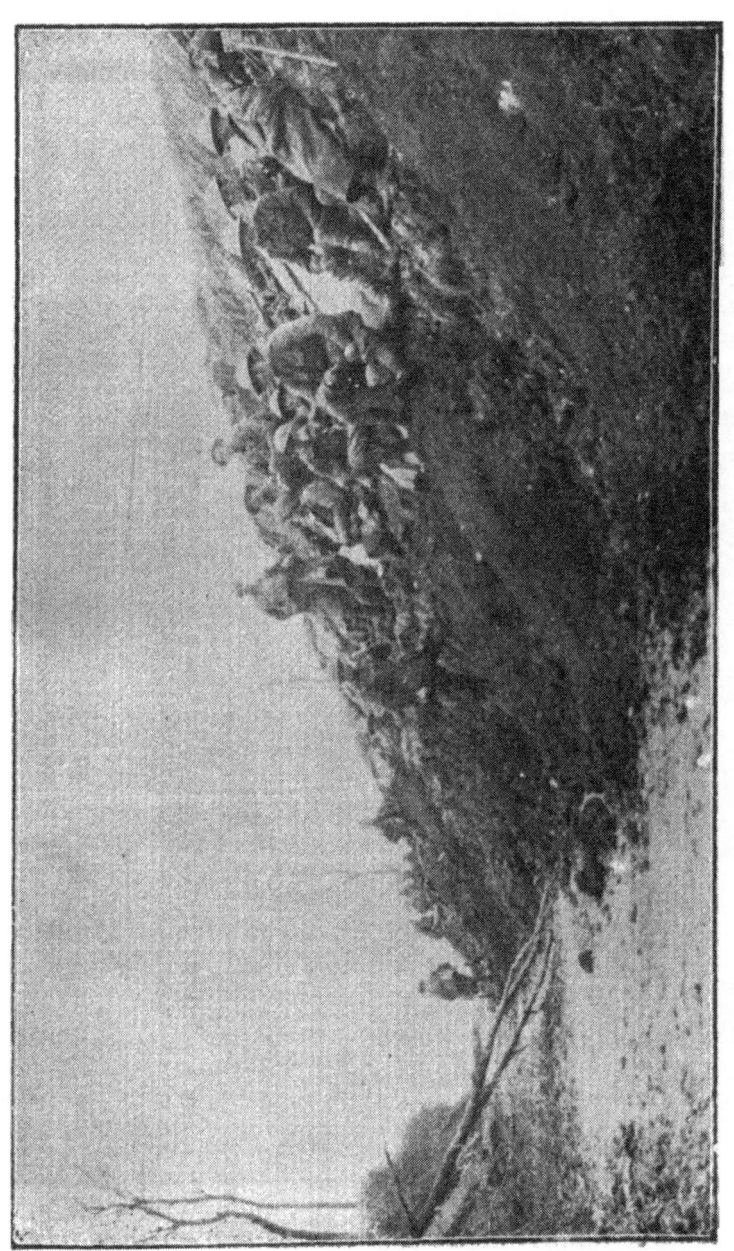

XIII.—THE EDGE OF MARRETT WOOD.

XIV.—CORBIE CATHEDRAL.

XV—VAUX WOOD AND THE ROAD LEADING TO CURLU.

XVI.—THE SOMME RIVER NEAR CORBIE.

HISTORY OF 38th BATTALION, A.I.F.

had been killed. Major Maudsley thereupon temporarily assumed command of the column, until Major Payne of the 40th Battalion was apprised of the situation when he took command.

Orders had been issued to the 37th Battalion to retire, and to effect this the 38th Battalion opened out astride the road. While rushing "D" Company up to move out into line with "B" Company its O.C., Capt. Orchard, in the darkness stumbled upon a bayonet which penetrated his leg causing him to be evacuated as a casualty. Lieut. Poole assumed charge of the Company.

It was a difficult matter to sight trenches in the darkness and obtain an idea of the enemy's positions. By 2.15 a.m. the Battalion had dug in sufficiently to make a determined stand. About 2.30 a.m. a memo, arrived from Brigade Headquarters to the effect that the 20th Battalion would attack at 4.30 a.m., to link up with our own supposed right at Avenue Cross.

This necessitated "C" Company, who had dug in south of the main road, evacuating and digging in as a support company in rear of outpost companies. When entrenched, the Battalion outpost line extended until it was linked up on the left with the 40th Battalion, continuing the line across the tram line. The general line faced the north-east.

The steadiness of the personnel of the Battalion was remarkable under such trying circumstances (those first wild moments would quickly have proved chaotic with undisciplined troops), and many excellent examples of coolness and courage were displayed. The tanks retired at 3.30 a.m., which was the signal for a further Hun outburst.

The Battalion Headquarters was now situated in a cellar at La Flaque cross roads. This spot was a particularly hot corner, being constantly under heavy shell and machine gun fire. When a shell took the end out of the building it was considered advisable to move, Headquarters being established in a Boche dugout at La Flaque dump.

Ration parties from the companies rendezvoued at the dump, where rations were delivered hot by the transport.

A heavy fog enveloped the countryside when morning broke on the 11th, and when the 20th Battalion went forward at 4.30 a.m. the roar of the artillery shut off all other sounds. Gas drifted over the area, and the fog held it down, necessitating the wearing of gas masks for a considerable time.

By 6.30 a.m. the 20th Battalion had come up in line on the right, although there was a gap of 700 yards between the 38th Battalion's right post and their left. "C" Company, under Capt. Dench was instructed to move south of the road and cover this gap; but about 7 a.m. a platoon of the 19th Battalion moved along the main road and formed a post along the south side, "C" Company extending beyond them. A machine gun section moving with the 20th Battalion was sent forward to cover this gap till the redistribution of the outpost line was accomplished.

As the fog gradually lifted it showed that "A" Company had dug in within 20 yards of a Boche strongpost. Privates T. G. Williams and J. W. H. Allit fired upon it until a white flag was displayed, when they rushed the post which yielded one officer, two N.C.O.'s and 15 other ranks as prisoners; another officer had been killed.

Privates Williams and Allit were afterwards awarded the Military Medal.

Later on a post of fourteen Boche surrendered to "D" Company, the surrender being due to the bravery and daring of Lance-Corporal J. G. Lewis and Pte. E. A. G. Smith, who hopped out of the trench and rushed the post, the determined rush of the gallant pair causing the Boche to "Kamerad." Their reward was also the Military Medal. Thus two dangerous nests of enemy machine guns were wiped out.

This latter operation of securing prisoners attracted the attention of the enemy, who opened out machine gun fire from the direction of Proyart on their own surrendering men, probably as a warning to other posts which might be contemplating a surrender.

The day was spent in shell holes and short trenches. These positions were shelled from time to time by a high velocity gun, the speed and weight of the projectiles giving the impression that the area was being bombed from above.

The night of the 11th passed in busy vigilance and work, the line being advanced and new outposts dug, strict watch being kept against enemy interference. Machine gun fire was now very intense, but it was remarkable that there was very little shelling. Enemy 'planes were very active, dropping bombs indescriminately over the whole area, favoring their own trenches as well as ours.

'Twas ludicrous to behold the enemy's lights going up when a bomb was dropped in his area. Our own posts adopted these tactics and secured a certain amount of immunity.

In the evening the Battalion was treated to a sideshow, a gorgeous firework display, when our artillery blew up a Boche Verey light dump. Firework displays along the enemy lines were common occurrences, for on the slightest suspicion of an attack vari-colored rockets would illuminate the area under suspicion. But on this occasion the blowing up of the Verey light dump, all previous displays paled to insignificance as box after box of gold, green and red lights soared skyward to burst with a radiance which put the sunset to shame.

The machine gun fire which had been intense throughout the night had completely ceased an hour before dawn. Platoon commanders in the front line put their heads together, and a message sent to the O.C. of "A" Company, Capt. F. E. Fairweather, M.C., speedily brought him to the spot. The Boche had evidently moved back; everything seemed to indicate it. On that supposition Captain Fairweather issued orders to No. 3 Platoon, under Lieut. C. H. Peters, M.C., to move out on a fighting patrol with a distant objective—Robert Wood, and Lieut. Schlitz, M.C. with a patrol to investigate posts along the main road.

The patrols were only out five minutes when No. 1 Platoon, under Lieut. D. Addison was also on the move.

With three Platoons in front and one in the rear "A" Company commenced the move which was to redeem the failure of the night of the 10th, and establish the Battle of Proyart as a Tenth Brigade success.

The Company advanced over undulating country, the scouts inspecting crops and protecting the flanks until after some casualties from machine gun fire from front and both flanks. Captain Fairweather established a line on a crest, when some rudimentary French trenches were occupied.

By this time the whole Battalion was on the move.

"C" Company made a most successful foray, a platoon fight when Lieut. F. H. Baxter and a party rushed a post, killing several of the garrison and taking the remainder prisoner. For his courage and daring Lieut. Baxter was awarded the Military Cross.

"B" Company took up a position in support, and "D" in reserve, and by the time the Companies had settled down in their new positions the whole Brigade was on the move.

From their coign of vantage "A" Company could look on and beyond the town of Proyart, and witnessed the stout resistance put up by the Boche against the 37th and 40th Battalions, particularly in Proyart and the dense wood beyond the town. Parties of the enemy were observed from time to time, and were dispersed by rifle and Lewis Gun. About midday the enemy commenced a bombardment of the area with an assortment of shells ranging from "whizz-bangs" to nine-point two's. This bombardment lasted until well on in the afternoon.

After nightfull, when all were worn out after a hard, hot day, came the cheering news of an early relief, and on the arrival of the 7th Battalion of the East Yorks, an impressively fine body of men, the Battalion moved back along the main road through scattered shelling to the old bivouacs in Hamilton Valley.

Among those who had laid down their lives in the fight for Proyart was Lieut. H. McColl, a well-known Bendigonian.

The 10th Brigade's daring attempt to cut off the enemy at Proyart had proved a splendid failure; an adventure entered upon with an "Aussie's" love for chance, and a reasonable assurance of success; a splendid failure which led to an ultimately successful operation. The enemy had suffered heavily, in lives, prisoners, and the loss of machine guns, and undoubtedly, the daring of the Australian at Proyart caused him to fear more than ever the nerve-racking and irresistible attacks which the "Diggers" continually launched upon him, driving him back, and gradually sapping his spirits, which were now in a very weak state. Knowing how badly the Boche had been punished and demoralised it was with no feeling of defeat that the 38th Battalion retired to Hamilton Valley, which was reached in the early part of August 13th. The day was spent in rest, so necessary after the strenuous days at Proyart. After a refreshing sleep a pic-nicing spirit prevailed. After a "stunt" the first impulse in these days of summer was to toss aside heavy clothing and loll about in the shade in short white underpants and open-necked shirts. The clear waters of the Somme proved a great attraction, and hot baths, if preferred, could be had on the river bank.

Perhaps the best reward for the work done at Proyart was an Australian mail and a large number of parcels which arrived towards evening.

A stay of nine days was made at Hamilton Valley. Training of a mild nature was carried out in the mornings, and the afternoons were devoted to recreation, and bootmakers' and tailors' parades.

Enemy bombing 'planes visited the area nightly, and dropped bombs on the chance of their falling in the gullies used for horse lines.

* * * *

CHAPTER VII.

THE FIGHTING FOR BRAY, CURLU, CLERY-SUR-SOMME AND ROISEL.

On 21st August the Battalion received orders to move to an area north of the Somme. The move was made that night in bright moonlight, and the route followed led through Cerissy, crossing the Somme at Chipilly, along the road into the Somme Valley to Sailly Laurette, and then north-east along the Morlancourt Road. The move was completed by one o'clock in the morning.

Here training was resumed for two days when a notification was received on 23rd that the Brigade would that night take over the line from the 9th Brigade.

The 38th Battalion took over the front line from the 33rd Battalion. "C" Company (Capt. Dench) was on the left; "D" Company (Lieut. Poole) on the right; "A" Company (Lieut. Addison) and "B" Company (Capt. Beattie) were in support.

On the following day the enemy commenced machine gun and artillery operations in the early hours of the morning and throughout the day heavily "strafed" the front line area from the direction of Mamits.

At 6.45 a.m. Capt. Dench of "C" Company, while bravely organising a stand on his left flank, where ground had been given by the 19th Division, was killed by a sniper.

On 24th August, the 37th and 40th Battalions pushed on through Bray and established posts east of the town, the 38th Battalion, right flank, conforming to the movement. Boche, in numerous parties, were observed opposite the Battalion front just forward of Ceylon Wood, commanding observation of all movements.

That night the Unit was relieved, when a move back was made to bivouacs, the Unit becoming reserve Battalion to the 10th Brigade in its attacks for the acquisition of high ground.

During the whole of the day the Battalion was subjected to intense artillery fire—all calibres of shells from 77 m.m. to 9in. being rained upon the area held by the Unit. The shelling began at 4.30 a.m. and did not slacken until 8 p.m., when it developed into the usual desultory shooting. The casualties for the day included one officer and five other ranks killed, and three officers and fifteen other ranks wounded.

On 26th August the Battalion moved forward, when "A" and "B" Companies pushed on, coming under control of 37th Battalion, "B" Company being sent forward to extend the line east of Suzanne to the River Somme.

During the early hours of the night "A", "B" and "C" Companies moved on to mop up the peninsula and establish a line and clear Royal Dragoons Wood. This work was accomplished without enemy opposition, and "A" Company established bridge head guards te Eclusier and Frise crossings.

The series of bridges connecting up with Curlu had been demolished by the retreating Boche, but were later repaired by the Third Australian Pioneers.

Work was received that the Battalion was to be relieved, but the relief was cancelled later in view of further hostile action by the Division.

Instructions were received from Brigade that the Battalion would work as a separate Unit under its Acting C.O., Major Maudsley. This necessitated a slight readjustment of Battalion dispositions.

The morning of 27th broke with light drizzling rain. Artillery, during the last 24 hours, had moved well up into position in Maricourt Valley, near Suzanne.

Patrols from "A" Company crossed the river at Eclusier and got into touch with the First Division; "'C' Company established a bridge head post guarding Vaux Bridge; and "B" Company captured, near Suzanne, a light minenwerfer and a heavy machine gun and carriage.

At 7.30 a.m. on 28th "B" Company was ordered to cross the river at Vaux Bridge and reconnoitre the peninsula on the opposite side of the river crossing. By noon the Company could be distinguished moving well out to the canal. The work of clearing the peninsula was accomplished with little or no interruption by the enemy, but at Frise bridgehead the Company had a lively time, coming under the fire of our own eighteen-pounders.

"C" and "D" Companies then moved out to attack from the line established by the 9th Brigade (it being stated that they had established a post slightly forward from Curlu towards the river) "D" Company moved through and on to the south of Curlu. As soon as this Company entered the town it met strong opposition, which was only subdued by determined and stubborn fighting on the Company's part.

During this action heavy casualties were sustained, but the Company succeeded in establishing a post 150 yards east of a bridgehead, the party chiefly responsible for the result being the platoon commanded by Lieut. Poole.

During the advance the Company inflicted many casualties on the enemy and captured four machine guns.

Through the night an advance was made, and later a further advance of 200 yards, was made by the whole Battalion, without opposition to an old line of German trenches to the east and in advance of Observation Wood.

In the early dawn of the 29th patrols pushed forward from the Companies and reconnoitred ground forward from Curlu. In Hindleg Wood an old German Headquarters was discovered. By midday they had captured the village of Hem, a mere heap of ruins, and were well on their way to Monacu.

Orders were given for a move on Clery-sur-Somme, the Battalion moving out at 11 a.m. in artillery formation covered by a troop of 13th Australian Light Horse.

From right to left were "A" "D" and "C" Companies, the right flank being the river, and the left flank of advance protected by the 40th Battalion, doing a flank guard. As the advance commenced the enemy put down a heavy curtain of shell fire, inflicting casualties, Lieut. Dutton, Lewis Gun officer, being killed.

The advance was continued along a ravine running east, which was lightly shelled. After a mile had been accomplished the Battalion came under heavy machine gun fire from three guns firing from the north. Here the cavalry screening the infantry suffered many casualties. Riders had their horses shot under them by the withering fire of the machine guns, which temporarily checked the advance, the infantry being forced to occupy a series of old trenches.

Pushing on again, after having obtained the assistance of the artillery, the attackers went over the brow of a hill which commanded a view of Clery, from where fire from eight machine guns caused another halt. These in their turn were dealt with by our own guns.

Again the Battalion advanced, and when crossing the railway line in a depression near Clery was heavily shelled.

The town was entered at dusk, two companies passing through it, searching for hidden Boche in the half light, and then pressing on to entrench for the night on an arranged line. The other companies then pressed on to this line east of Clery, the left flank being east of Copse 5B, the line running towards the river.

The Unit had been fighting for 84 hours, and everyone was worn out. With the arrival of rations, a good hot meal, spirits revived, and everyone settled down for a much-needed rest, the 37th Battalion having passed on to continue the attack.

Since 2 p.m. on August 26th the Battalion had secured by fighting a depth of 9000 yards from the enemy. Holding ground won, and acting as reserve Battalion to the Brigade, the Unit awaited orders for the next move.

At 7.30 on the evening of 30th August, Battalion Commanders were called to a conference to discuss the continuation of the attack, the objective of which was the trench system running N.W. The dispositions for the attack were, 38th Battalion to be on the right, the 39th on the left, to take over from 37th Battalion. Throughout the day and night the Battalion was subjected to heavy shelling and machine gun fire. The move to relieve the 37th Battalion and continue attacking was completed by 4.20 a.m. on 31st, when the Battalion settled down to await the barrage which was to commence at 6 a.m.

The final instructions for the attack were received by Company commanders at 5.25, having been received from Brigade Headquarters as late as 3.30 a.m. At 5.30 the enemy opened up a heavy shoot on the front line and valley.

At 6 o'clock the Battalion advanced under a barrage and when within 50 yards of the trenches just vacated, strong enemy opposition was encountered, and much hand-to-hand fighting ensued. Very destructive machine gun fire came from the direction of Clery Copse, and it was here that Corporal (now Sergeant) A. V. Grinton won the Distinguished Conduct Medal for courageous work on the left flank. With a few men he rushed an enemy machine gun and captured its gunners, thus saving a weak flank heavily attacked. He also helped a composite patrol that captured three pieces of enemy field artillery, eight machine guns, and killed numbers of enemy, finally capturing 25 unwounded prisoners.

The enemy troops which the Battalion encountered were Queen Augusta's Grenadier Guards, who, it was said, volunteered in Berlin to come up and stop the advance of the Australians. But the swift and determined advance of the "Diggers" unnerved the Guards who quickly "Kameraded." There was one Australian to every ten yards, and through them the crestfallen Guards passed, as prisoners, literally in hundreds.

It was noticed that they all wore brand new uniforms and equipment, which showed that they were new troops.

On swept the Battalion, down a hill and into Van Trench and up over the next hill to Berlin Wood. The objective (The Red Line) Inferno Trench, Zombo Trench, Morava Trench, was reached at 7.15 a.m.

Numbers of the enemy were found in several trenches, but they gladly surrendered, having no desire to fight. Scarcely had the new positions been consolidated when a warning was received of a counter attack on the left flank by about 120 of the enemy.

A party from "C" Company formed a defensive flank and fire was opened out on the attackers, who took to trenches. Again they came on, attempting to bomb their way through, but were heavily repelled, and the survivors retired through trenches to the opposite hillside.

Shortly after the Battalion had reached its objective, Lieut. Baxter led a patrol forward about 800 yards, and with Lewis Gun fired upon a German field piece, killing its crew.

Parties of the enemy observed him and attempted to cut off the patrol by outflanking it, thus forcing his retirement. For this cool and courageous work Lieut. Baxter was awarded a bar to his Military Cross, won at Proyart.

The Battalion was now holding a line from the Canal-du-Nord on the south to a trench junction.

Many heroic deeds had been performed to win through to the objective, and many casualties, both killed and wounded, had been sustained. Major A. J. A. Maudsley, Acting C.O., had been killed by a bursting shell, at 6.30 a.m., the control of the attacking Battalion then falling on the shoulders of the Acting Adjutant, Lieut. H. R. Robbins, who shouldered his manifold duties with promptitude and ability. At 10 a.m. word had been received that Colonel R. O. Henderson, D.S.O., commanding the 39th Battalion, would take the dual command of the two Battalions (38th and 39th), but the Colonel, just recovering from a bout of influenza, had virtually to allow Lieut. Robbins to carry the direction of the 38th Battalion on his shoulders. It was for this and other fine work that Lieut. Robbins was afterwards awarded the Military Cross.

Two other officers to win the Military Cross were Lieuts. J. F. Eason and N. W. W. Sandiford.

Lieut. Eason had a few days earlier rushed a machine gun post on a bridge crossing the Somme at Curlu, and by a determined dash he and his platoon captured two guns, one light and one heavy.

Lieut. Sandiford, who took over the command of "B" Company when Captain L. J. Beattie was wounded, completed the task of clearing the peninsula between Vaux Wood and Feueillers, and later on, at Clery, on August 31st, led his Company to its objective and there consolidated, and although wounded remained on duty for 12 hours, until finally he was forced by exhaustion to give in and evacuate the firing line.

At 11.30 p.m. word was received that the Unit would be relieved by the 43rd Battalion moving through at 5 o'clock next morning, September 1st, under the protection of a barrage. In the meantime the enemy was heavily shelling with gas and high explosive, both on the hill and in the valley in rear. Battalion Headquarters was at this time situated in Van Trench on the forward slope of a ridge overlooking Berlin Copse.

The 43rd Battalion passed through the 38th Battalion at the arranged time and disappeared in the heavy fog and mist of the morning.

The relief was through in the forward area at 6.30 a.m. the barrage having prevented "A" and "B" Companies from moving out at an earlier hour.

The Battalion moved back to bivouacs in the vicinity of Curlu, where the Rev. Frank Hanlon and his Y.M.C.A. staff had toiled through the night in preparation for the coming of the worn-out fighters. Hot cocoa, biscuits, and cigarettes awaited them, and later on a good hot meal was served up by the Battalion cooks after which everyone settled down for a well-earned and much-needed sleep.

HISTORY OF 38th BATTALION, A.I.F. 73

Four days were spent in this area in rest, cleaning up, and reorganising as a fighting Unit, and on the evening of 5th September, in accordance with an order from Brigade Headquarters the Battalion moved forward. En route a heavy thunderstorm swept down upon the long column (enveloped in clouds of dust disturbed by heavy traffic on the roads) and in a few minutes everyone was wet through. The roads soon became very slippery, and hundreds of heavy motor lorries, unable to make any progress up the slippery inclines, held up the transport traffic for miles back. By 8 p.m. the Battalion reached bivouacs, everyone's spirits being damped by the weather and the uncomfortable march.

On the following day advance parties from Battalion Headquarters and Companies moved forward to reconnoitre the forward area held by the 11th Brigade the line battalion of which was then fighting for Tincourt. All the villages and camps on from Clery-sur-Somme had been systematically destroyed by the retreating Hun, and many "Booby traps" had been discovered by various Units. " 'Twas wise to be wary" in this area. A half-closed door of a building or dugout if opened might explode a mine. To an innocent-looking shovel stuck in the ground might be attached a fine wire, perhaps covered with earth, connecting up with a few pounds of high explosive. The Boche had always been noted for his sunning; he was devilishly cunning when it came to setting "Booby traps." And so every precaution was necessary when passing through or occupying his late positions.

On 7th September the Battalion moved on again ready to take over the line held by the 41st Battalion. The outpost line was supposed to run east of Roisel and Hervilly.

Moving on to take up this line the Battalion's progress was not impeded by the enemy. When passing through Roisel the town was heavily shelled, but no casualties were sustained; and when crossing Cologne Valley the enemy shelled that neighborhood. Here and there villages were burning (fired by the Hun) from whence dense columns of smoke curled skyward.

The guides supplied by the outgoing Battalion lost their direction and it was not until 4 a.m. that the relief was completed. Lieut.-Colonel Hurry, D.S.O. (38th Batt.) commanded the vanguard troops, comprising which were 37th and 38th Battalions, A.I.F.; 10th Australian Light Trench Mortar Battery, two sections of 10th Machine Gun Company, and one troop of 13th Australian Light Horse, supported by artillery. The 37th Battalion operated on the right, 38th Battalion on the left; the right flank of the British Division operating on our left was the 24th Welsh Regiment. On the right flank was the 29th Battalion A.I.F. The 38th was responsible for approximately 3000 yards frontage, the 37th Battalion for 2500 yards.

At dawn on the 8th it was found that the Blue Line had not been occupied by the relieved Vanguard, and orders were issued by the C.O. to gradually push forward to the outpost line under the protection of the Light Horse. This was successfully accomplished by 9 p.m., the enemy's scattered machine gun fire scarcely interfering with the movement. The 40th Battalion then moved through and established a line in an old trench system running north and south, the 38th Battalion then automatically becoming support battalion to the vanguard.

The dawn of September 9th ushered in a bleak wind which throughout the day caused much physical inconvenience, the troops being without blankets and packs.

Next day advance parties from the 1st A.I.F. Division visited the area to take over the operations of the vanguard, the 3rd and 4th Battalions taking over the outpost line.

That night the 38th Battalion was relieved, and moved back to hutments near Mont St. Quentin.

While moving back, hostile bombing 'planes were exceptionally active, but, fortunately, the Unit did not suffer by their operations.

A rest period of 18 days was made at a very pleasantly situated camp near Mont St. Quentin. After a good rest the first attraction was the hot baths at Doingt.

Mild training was carried out in the mornings, principally for Lewis gunners, who were also instructed in the use of enemy machine guns, two of the guns captured from the enemy being retained for this purpose.

The Battalion's popular and energetic "Padre" (Captain-Chaplain Freer) organised several concerts from local talent. These entertainments were a great success, and were thoroughly enjoyed by all. In these days the Australian Divisions were not separated by distance, as in the earlier days of the war. The result was that friends and relatives met again after long years of fighting.

In the many camps scattered for miles around the men from various Divisions and Brigades gathered together to discuss the days gone by, the present hopeful situation, and the bright future, the dawn of which was now breaking.

A mile away from the camp occupied by the 38th Battalion lay the shattered town of Peronne, surrounded by mounds of brick dust, where once had stood small villages.

The enemy was not content to leave this area in peace, for nightly his Gothas purred overhead, and their bombs crashed out from time to time.

But soon these nocturnal excursions were checked by anti-aircraft gunners and by our own 'planes, which patrolled the air ready to tackle the Gothas once they were caught by the broad beams of the searchlights. On several occasions the area was lit up by Gothas brought to earth in flames, when cheering for miles around was heard in the quiet of the night.

About midday stores for the Canteen would arrive when a long queue would be quickly formed. Great difficulty was often experienced in obtaining goods such as tobacco, cigarettes and preserved fruits, for which there was a never-ending demand; but Sergt. Rangecroft and his assistants were to be complimented for the manner in which they toiled to successfully meet this demand. It was no small task to provide smokes and one hundred and one odds and ends for a battalion of men whose appetites for something tasty, to relieve the monotony of army rations, seemed insatiable.

During the Battalion's activities at the front one of the things that helped in no small degree to lighten the hearts of all was the Band. Though it could not continue as a fighting unit and remain intact at the same time, for the first seven months of the Battalion's entry into the battle line the members of the Band were engaged in stretcher-bearing and trench warfare. Right up to the end of the battle of Messines bandsmen had been the first to come to the aid of the Battalion's casualties, as well as in every raid or stunt which occurred. Unfortunately, it was inevitable that such a body could not carry on without sustaining casualties. In the trenches before Armentieres, and in the several successful raids that occurred on that sector, the Band sustained five casualties, two being killed. Reinforcements for stretcher-bearing had to be obtained from the Companies, and following the Battalion's entry into the Ploegsteert sector, a few weeks before the great Messines victory it was becoming evident that in a short time the Band would be "napoo." However, it struggled on, and one Sunday morning, in the heart of the Ploegsteert Wood, with the enemy in easy hearing distance, the remaining members of the Band attended a Church Parade, when for the last time for many weeks it was able to render the necessary music.

The raids preceding the victory of Messines caused another serious depletion amongst the remaining personnel of the Band, when two more players were killed and four wounded. At the great battle of Messines Ridge four more of the Band were casualties.

It is hardly necessary at this stage to describe particular incidents, or to give any general account of the work done by the Band on the battlefield. Every man of the Battalion who remembers those first few months will acknowledge the fact that nothing was too much when first-aid was needed for a fallen comrade. This fact was emphasised at the first Battalion Parade held after the taking of Messines, when out of a band of 25 members only six men and the Bandmaster were on parade. It could be mentioned here that the Band had also sustained casualties amongst instruments, several of which have been hit by enemy shell fire.

Many weeks went by before the Band could be brought up to its former strength. The authorities recognised the value of regimental bands, and every effort was made to bring instrumentalists to the Band, and also to keep it intact for the future, or as long as the fortunes of war would allow.

An incident is worth recalling which occurred on the night after the Battalion marched forward to stem the German onrush before Amiens. The Bandsmen were called upon to carry tea up to their hungry comrades, so many being told off for each Company. It was a dark night, the distance was unknown, and vague directions were given as to the Battalion's exact location. However, three Companies received their long-looked-for tea in due time, but "B" Company had still a long time to wait. At that time there was a very uncertain feeling in everyone's mind as to what was going to happen, but to those few who were engaged in carrying full dixies for "B" Company over paddocks, hills and ploughed land, in the middle of the night, in the hope of eventually running up against something or someone, that peculiar feeling was intensified to a practical certainty that something was going to happen. Not a sound could be heard—not even a Verey light was seen—that would give any indication of the whereabouts of either friend or foe. One of the party said it could not be much further before striking the German frontier; another suggested sending a runner back with a report that a wide gap had been made in the enemy's line, and to send Light Horse immediately. However, all speculations and suggestions were suddenly cut short by a loud challenge to halt. It was said in good English, and the voice came, it seemed, from the ground. Someone in rear asked in a whisper whether anyone knew German. But the next words of the sentry were in the reassuring and unmistakable "Aussie lingo," and the party advanced to find themselves on to their own Battalion's trenches, arriving there not from the rear, but from the front!

Many more incidents could be recorded, and much interesting matter might be written of the Band's welfare since its formation at Bendigo were space available. The upkeep of a regimental band, and its general efficiency musically while on active service is a difficult and often a discouraging task. Music, especially when performed by a number together, cannot be expected to be rendered perfectly during such a rough and severe experience as active service really is; notwithstanding all such difficulties, the 38th Band under the conductorship since its formation in Australia of Sergeant J. J. Code, never failed in its best endeavors to lighten the hearts of those who were passing through the nerve-racking strain and hardships of this great struggle for freedom, safety and justice.

The rest period spent at Mont St. Quentin will always be remembered as a very happy time.

At 6.30 p.m. on 27th September, the Battalion moved to bivouacs in rear of Ronssoy Wood. The route taken led through Busu, Templeux-la-Fosse Longavesnes, Villers-Faucon, and St. Emilie.

In these days, when the enemy was being pressed back to his old quarters in the Hindenburg line, along the dusty roads, endless streams of traffic, artillery, transport sections and infantry were pushing forward through the shattered villages and camps lately occupied by the enemy.

Dumps of war material which he had been unable to take with him lay at the road-side here and there; everywhere his notices greeted one from signposts, and afforded a certain amount of interest to passing troops. "Gott Strafe England," and other affectionate greetings were chalked in large letters on the walls of buildings, and one optimistic Hun artist had sketched His Majesty King George kneeling before the Kaiser and holding a lighted match for the All Highest's cigar. One imagined that the artist had done this rather clever work when he had advanced through that village in March.

CHAPTER VIII.

THE BATTALION'S LAST FIGHT.

Through varying scenes of devastation the Battalion marched to Ronssoy Wood, arriving there at 2 a.m. on 28th September. Tea was provided shortly after arrival at the new area, but a much-needed rest was disturbed throughout the early hours of the morning by a heavy bombardment of gas and high explosive shells, and enemy bombing 'planes.

A 10 a.m. a conference of Battalion commanders was held at Brigade Headquarters, and orders for the next operation were issued. The day passed away quietly, the troops making up for sleep lost during the hours of shelling. In the afternoon the route towards the Brown Line was reconnoitred by a selected party.

At 5.30 on the following morning, Sunday 29th September, the members of the 38th Battalion crawled out of their "bivvies" to prepare for what was to eventually prove their last fight in the greatest of all wars; a battle which was to be fought along a wide front and smash the defences of the famous Hindenburg Line, and drive the enemy back, causing him a few weeks' afterwards to cry out for peace.

All were well acquainted with the nature of the "stunt" which was, in brief, to follow the Americans through the Hindenburg line to their objective, known as the Green Line, then to exploit their success, pushing through them for a distance of about four kilometres and there consolidate, this to be done without the aid of a barrage, and under open warfare conditions.

The barrage which was put down on the enemy to assist the Americans to advance opened out at 5.50 a.m. and the result of this, as far as the Battalion was concerned, was that its position was heavily "strafed" by enemy gas shells.

The Battalion's move forward was timed for 7.15 a.m., so between six o'clock and that time it was subjected to gas, with the result that nearly all hands were sick, and many became casualties. The "Fall in" was extremely difficult in consequence of the shelling and on account of gas masks being worn. Moving off in column of route, "A" Company (Captain F. E. Fairweather, M.C.) led, followed by Battalion Headquarters (Lieut.-Colonel G. Hurry, D.S.O.); then came "C" Company (Captain C. H. Peters. M.C.), followed by "B" (Lieut. J. B. O'Donnell) and "D" Company (Captain W. J. Collins).

The route to be taken to the Brown Line was as follows:— South of the village of Ronssooy to cross roads, then through Orchard Post to Bellecourt Road, thence north-easterly to Guillemont Farm, where tanks, as had been arranged, would meet to co-operate with the Battalion.

Arriving on high ground clear of the gas it was a great relief to remove the suffocating gas masks, and drink in the clear morning air.

From here the morning was revealed in all its beauty; the sun shone out, and the atmosphere was pure and fresh. The landscape was truly magnificent, the country stretching out in gentle undulations, the hollows being filled with gas and smoke which created beautiful cloud effects.

It was not long before it was necessary to adopt artillery formation, the advance being now made over very rough country and through many belts of wire.

At about 8 a.m. the Unit passed through the artillery batteries which were shooting the barrage for the Americans, and much to everyone's surprise suddenly realised that it was at this early hour under enemy machine gunfire.

A fine spectacle was here witnessed, that of an enemy 'plane (Red Devil type) flying quite low and dropping signals for guidance to enemy artillery. For quite a long time this "devil" hovered about, being fired at by machine gunners from all points until at last it was hit in a vital part and crashed to earth amid cheering of many troops.

The advance continued until Pot Trench was reached, when the Battalion was held up by machine gun fire coming from the direction of Bony. All were at a loss to know what had happened, for if all had gone well the Americans would be well ahead and there should be no resistance of this nature at this stage. The machine gun fire steadily increased.

The leading Company ("A"), which had been held up in Dog Trench, pushed on again in an attempt to clear up the situation and advanced in half sectional rushes from shell hole to shell hole. At 9.50 a.m. "C" Company moved on and occupied their late position, to suffer many casualties from heavy shelling.

"B" Company then took up a position in Cat Post with "D" Company on their left.

Numbers of Americans, many of whom were wounded, came filtering back to the Battalion's positions and were barraged with questions. Each answer was the same; they had lost their leaders and did not know where they had been or what had been done; none could give the information required. The only conclusion which could be made was that the Americans had lost their barrage, which, sweeping ahead according to plan, had exposed their troops to the fire of machine gunners and riflemen, who had found ample time after the barrage lifted to come out of their dugouts and prepare their defence. This meant that the Americans must have failed to accomplish their task of gaining their objective. This conclusion was later on confirmed when the Battalion passed through lines of American dead mown down by enemy machine gunners and snipers.

From the position held by "C" Company in Dog Trench numbers of tanks could be seen, put out of action by the enemy. These were in some cases on fire, and from nearly all came smoke.

Very little information was being obtained as to the progress of "A" Company. "C" Company then sent forward a small patrol, but it almost immediately became casualties. Captain C. H. Peters. M.C., went out later and located "A" Company's headquarters in a shell hole about 100 yards east of Dog Trench, the remainder of the Company having consolidated positions in shell holes within 50 yards of the wire in front of South Guillemont Trench.

At 11 a.m. it was reported that Captain F. E. Fairweather, M.C. and Bar, had been seriously wounded in the neck, and Lieut. Callan had been killed. Later, news came back that Captain Fairweather had died about ten minutes after being hit, and that Lieut. J. L. Whitehead was now in charge of "A" Company.

The death of the Company's O.C. was a severe loss to the Battalion. Captain Fairweather was one of the Units most capable officers, a cool, level-headed soldier, and a fearless fighter.

At 12.30 information was received that the Americans were everywhere in the Green Line, and that the machine guns holding up the Battalion were a few they had failed to mop up. The Unit, together with the 39th and 40th Battalion, was to move forward and get in touch with the Americans. At 3 p.m. the advance was continued. "C" Company moved out of Dog Trench and pushed forward from shell hole to shell hole under exceptionally heavy machine gun fire and shelling, to suffer many casualties. At 4 p.m. the Company's advance was checked by the broad belt of wire west of South Guillemont Trench. The few gaps in the wire were under machine gun barrage from the enemy, who also had snipers covering these gaps. These conditions rendered further progress impossible, so the assistance of the artillery was called for. Soon our batteries became active and were successful in silencing many of the machine guns and minenwerfer. Tanks were then sent for and they trundled up on their hazardous task; but it was not long before they were put out of action. A smoke screen was then requested, which was put down in the valley ahead and proved most effective, enabling "A" and "C" Companies to push forward, without being observed, to the South Guillemont Trench, which had been evacuated by the enemy, excepting a few of his wounded, who were taken prisoner. Posts were quickly established and were manned by "Yanks" and "Diggers" combined. The right post "C" Company was established in touch with the 41st Battalion on the left; "A" Company established a post. The trench was cleared and made as comfortable, and as safe from enemy shells as was possible.

At 7 p.m. Battalion Headquarters moved up. The night was extremely rough, being wet, windy and very cold. All hands were in rather low spirits on account of not knowing how things were actually progressing. At 9 p.m. the cheering news was passed along to send back to Dog Trench for rations. In an hour's time all were busily eating a hearty meal. At 3.30 a.m. the morning meal arrived, together with a good supply of cigarettes and matches.

At 4.30 a.m. (September 30th) orders were received that the 11th Brigade, with two battalions of the 9th Brigade, would attack at 6 a.m. on a battalion frontage in a northerly direction, and take up a line running to the Knob. The 10th Brigade was to clear up Claymore Valley and push on toward Bony.

At 6.30 a.m. the advance was continued, and to the apparent disappointment of the Americans orders were received that they were not to accompany the Battalion. "B" Company pushed through "A" and "C" Companies and took up a position in Claymore Trench and during this operation captured four Hotchkiss guns, taken by the enemy from a disabled tank.

"A" and "C" Companies moved forward up Bread Lane and consolidated in Claymore Trench; "D" Company being in support in Dog Trench.

At 9.50 a.m. "C" Company pushed forward again by way of Bony Avenue to a point on the crest of the hill which commanded an extensive view of Bony village and the surrounding country, including the Hindenburg system of trenches.

A patrol from the Company made an attempt to advance, but was checked by machine gun fire from the village. Luckily it succeeded in withdrawing without sustaining a casualty.

The enemy commanded all approaches and was able to engage attacking forces at 800 yards, thus affording the small Company, its strength now sadly reduced, no chance in the unequal fight.

"D" Company had now moved up to South Guillemont Trench, and established its headquarters.

Great satisfaction was expressed when the signallers arrived at "C" Company's position with their apparatus, having laid a wire which connected with Battalion Headquarters. The Company was now able to send back much valuable information on account of their splendid position from where enemy movements could be observed.

At 6 p.m. it was reported from Brigade Headquarters by 'phone that in the morning the 10th Brigade would co-operate with the 9th Brigade on the right and push forward, possibly as far as the Knob; definite orders were to follow later. "C" Company's post in Bony Avenue was, on account of being detached. then withdrawn to Claymore Trench. But at 8.30 p.m. the order for the proposed Brigade operation was cancelled. During the night patrols went forward, but were unable to gain any information. At 6 a.m. (October 1st) "C" Company re-established the post in Bony Avenue, and at 8.35 a.m. pushed in round the north of the village across the Le Catelet Canal, and there encountered a very determined resistance, a patrol of a neighboring Company being decimated. In the meantime "B" Company had followed to mop up the village.

"C" Company, now only 20 strong, dug in with the 39th Battalion on their left and 33rd Battalion on their right and consolidated this new line.

At 2.30 p.m. orders were received that the 37th Battalion would push forward and occupy the Knob, with the left flank on the Canal Tunnel end. The 40th Battalion would push out and occupy Bony Point, in touch with the 37th on the left and right flank of the Brigade right boundary. The 39th and 38th Battalions would be disposed in the main Hindenburg system as supports to the 37th and 40th Battalions respectively. At 3 p.m., positions as above were established, with the exception that the 39th Battalion carried out the task of the 40th Battalion, and vice versa. The dispositions of the 38th Battalion were at this time as follows:—

"B" and "C" Companies in that portion of the Hindenburg Line known as A 15 b, "A" Company in Bony Avenue, and "D" Company in support; Battalion Headquarters was now established at A13c. While "D" Company was taking up its new position Captain W. J. Collins, O.C., was badly wounded.

XVII.—38th BATTALION BAND AND APPRECIATIVE AUDIENCE, HAMILTON WOOD.

XVIII.—"C" COMPANY IN DOG TRENCH, HINDENBERG LINE.

Lieut. E. Potter then took charge of the Company and directed its movements in an able manner.

The Battalion now being in support, was able to seek a much-needed rest when several of the huge dugouts in the Hindenburg system were occupied. These dugouts were wonderful caverns, deep and concreted and able to accommodate whole battalions. Here all felt as safe from shell fire as if hundreds of miles from the line. The only danger which at first presented itself was the possibility of their being mined, but a careful examination by engineers dissolved that fear.

On reaching the Hindenburg Line one had experienced a great feeling of elation, together with a sense of disappointment in regard to the construction of the trenches from an engineering point of view. One had pictured these trenches as being tremendously elaborate, but on beholding them their main features proved to be difficult wire entanglements, deep trenches, and huge dugouts.

On the following day (October 2nd) the Battalion's positions were maintained. Enemy artillery was moderately active, particularly in the vicinity of Bony.

After 12.15 p.m. the welcome news of an early relief was received, the 10th Brigade's positions to be taken over by the 151st Brigade, B.E.F.

In accordance with the order received, the 38th Battalion was to withdraw to the old bivouacs in the rear of Ronssoy Wood. The withdrawal commenced at 4.30 p.m. and was complete at 5.45 p.m. On arrival at the Wood a good hot meal awaited the Battalion, and after it had been enjoyed by hungry, tired men, all crept back into those little bivouacs which had been deserted on the morning of September 22nd, while men passed through Hell's gate. Many had not returned to their bivouacs. One face in particular was missed; the cheery face of the Battalion's Padre, Chaplain-Captain Freer. He had last beee seen helping out the wounded. Now he was posted as missing. But great was the joy expressed by all when, afterwards it was discovered that he was still in the land of the living; but the feeling of joy was slightly marred by the fact that the "Padre" had lost one of his merry eyes through the bursting of a shell.

Among those who fell in the fight for the Hindenburg Line was Lieutenant-Colonel R. O. Henderson, commanding the 39th Battalion. Great sorrow was expressed when the news of his death reached the 38th Battalion. Lieut.-Colonel Henderson sailed from Australia with the 38th Battalion, and in February, 1917, was appointed to command the 39th Battalion.

Throughout the whole of the Division he was admired as a clever and fearless leader, and was idolized by his men.

Many heroic deeds had been performed; the Battalion winning further honors. The Unit's Quartermaster (Lieutenant P. J. Telfer) being awarded the Military Cross, and Captain C. H. Peters a bar to his Military Cross. Nine Military Medals were won by the N.C.O.'s and men. (See appendix.) Sergeant E. S. Beard, of the Transport Section, winning a bar to his medal won at Ypres.

Thus ends the account of how a mere handful of tired Australians took up a fight after regiments of brave Americans had been cut up, and their settled plan had been foiled; and how these same "Aussies", suffering heavy casualties, fought with skill, endurance, and tenacity a four days' battle; captured a section of the Hun's much-vaunted Hindenburg Line; captured the village of Bony; crossed the famous Le Catalet Canal and held a rapidly-dug line until other troops passed through them and continued the victorious advance which was to quickly bring peace which the whole world eagerly awaited after four long years of terrific and ghastly warfare.

Before turning in for the night it had been announced that on the following day a competition would be held, to be won by the dirtiest man in the Battalion. After four days' struggle when one's daily toilet was completely forgotten, it will be readily imagined that this competition was not to be easily judged. However, Corporal "Joe" Foster, of "B" Company, looking like a cave man of pre-historic days, and wearing a fierce growth of beard which vainly strove to hide the smiles wreathing his genial "Aussie dial," walked off triumphant.

*   *   *   *

CHAPTER IX.

"THE TRAIL THAT LEADS TO HOME."

On October 3rd, the Battalion moved from Ronssoy Wood to the vicinity of Aizecourt. Resting here until the 5th an order arrived from Brigade to the effect that the Unit was to move back to a rest near Abbeville. Moving on a light railway conveyed the Battalion to Peronne, from where it moved to an entraining point at Flamicourt. Entraining here at 4.15 in the afternoon, Pont Remy was reached just before midnight, and after a four mile march the quiet little villages of Bellifontaine and Bailleul accommodated the tired troops. "A" and "B" Companies billeting in the former village, and "C" and "D" Companies with Battalion Headquarters at Bailleul. Daylight revealed a picturesque neighborhood, a green valley which Autumn had commenced to color with her magic brush. The apple orchards held a canopy of yellow leaves above the green grass; and in the woods richer tints splashed the leaves of trees and climbers. After long months of fighting in torn and devastated areas what a delight and a relief it was to gaze upon green rounded hills, the orchards where late rosy apples still clung to the trees, and the gorgeous woods; all untouched by the marring hand of war. All war's attendant strains immediately fell from one's shoulders, a burden gladly dropped at the roadside and quickly forgotten as one turned aside to wander in peace through fields and woods.

A stay of eighteen days was made in this neighborhood. Mild training was carried out, and the Battalion was reorganised on a four company basis. These were busy days for the bootmakers, tailors, and barber, for after many weeks of hard work up in the line, clothing, boots and hair were in a ragged condition. In these days the daily newspapers were rushed.

Germany, baffled and beaten, was crying out for an armistice which would lead to an early peace; so it will easily be imagined how war-weary men feverishly read the daily columns, often, perhaps, sceptically, for even those who knew that the Hun was badly beaten found it hard to realise that the long struggle would soon be over.

On October 14th instructions were received from high authority that the 37th Battalion would organise as two Companies and amalgamate with the 38th Battalion. The personnel from the 37th would form "A" and "B" Companies of the 38th whose personnel would form "C" and "D" Companies. "A" and "B" Companies of the 38th Battalion amalgamated to form new "C" Company, "C" and "D" Companies formed new "D" Company.

On October 18th the Unit moved to billets at Sorel and Wanel, villages about four miles distant from Bailleul. The Transport Section remained on at Bailleul owing to the scarcity of water in the other villages.

On the morning of the 19th the Battalion was inspected by the Acting Brigadier (Lieut.-Colonel Jess). Light rains and cold weather now set in, but the days were brightened by intermittent sunshine. A Brigade sports meeting was held on 26th October in the neighborhood of Hocquincourt, the championship being won by the 10th Field Ambulance.

Football practice was now in full swing, and a complete Divisional programme of matches was arranged. This competition commenced on 2nd November, when the 38th Battalion defeated the 3rd Div. Signal School at Hallencourt.

Another keenly contested match played against the 39th Battalion on 9th November resulted in a win for that Unit.

On Monday, 11th, a telegram was received from Brigade, which stated that an armistice had been signed by the belligerent armies.

It was surprising how quietly the news was received. When one had struggled on through long years of bitter warfare, which at times had seemed a never-ending business, it was difficult to grasp the wonderful fact that at last the curtain had been lowered on the world's hideous drama, and that victory—a Glorious Victory—was the Allies' reward for their dogged stand (often at times against huge odds), and their persistent attacks of the past three months.

On the 10th day of December the Battalion again moved to take up fresh quarters in Vismes-au-val, Oisement area. Liberal leave to the United Kingdom, Paris and to Italy, was now being granted, and also to the surrounding towns and villages. Abbeville, the town so loved by Ruskin for its architectural beauties, proved a great attraction.

Mr. W. D. Craufurd, in "Peeps Into Picardy," says:—"The Ambaine were probably the first inhabitants of this district, and on the appearance of the Romans took refuge on an island in the Somme, which became a place of defence for them, and later on the actual site of the city. Ceasar held these people in great admiration on account of their bravery. From the conquest of Julius Caesar until the invasion of the Franks, Ponthieu remained under the dominion of the Emperors, and was called "Abbatis Villa." The domination of the Romans can be seen by the number of vast entrenchments in the country around, especially at Liercourt and in the neighborhood of St. Valery. They have quite modified the aspect of the countryside. These camps were evidently destined to defend the banks of the Somme against the attacks of the Northern Belgians. Some historians hold that it was in this river that Caesar collected the large Flotilla with which he made his second expedition to great Britain.

The district of Abbeville is the richest in antiquities in the Department; it is traversed from east to north by an ancient road, called Brunehault Grand Chemin, or La Chaussee Brunehault, after the mother of Clothaire I., whose name was Brunehault. This road passes through Noyelles-en-Chaussee, Estrees and Le Crecy. There is reason to believe that it is part of the great Roman Road from Lyon to Boulogne-sur-Mer, via Amiens, which, on Strabo's authority, was constructed by order of the Emperor Augustus."

"In the Fifth Century, a horde of Barbarians, as they were called, from Germany, fell as a thunderbolt upon this portion of the Roman Empire, dealing destruction on all sides, until, in the IXth Century, this once-important town was reduced to a mere farm, belonging to the great neighboring Abbey of St. Riquier.

"Since then, and particularly in later centuries, the tables have been turned, for Abbeville is now the important city, St. Riquier, having degenerated into a quiet and almost deserted village, beautifully situated, and surrounded by the glories of its past."

Ruskin, in his "Proeterita," says:—"For cheerful, unalloyed, unwearying pleasure, the getting in sight of Abbeville on a fine summer afternoon, jumping out in the courtyard of the Hotel de l'Europe, and rushing down the street to see St. Wulfram before the sun was off the towers, are things to cherish the past for—to the end."

The church of St. Wulfram is a magnificent specimen of Gothic style, flanked by two suburb Gothic towers. Several other churches in Abbeville are worthy of careful examination, especially that of St. Sepulchre and St. Giles. The town boasts many ancient buildings, and has an old-world charm which takes one's thoughts step by step back through those centuries crowded with romance.

Twelve miles north-east of Abbeville lies the picturesque little town of Crecy, where was fought one of the greatest battles of ancient times. Its main street is flanked by trees and quaint houses, and in the Place du Marche are two memorials of the battle—a red brick column surmounted by a small cross erected by the English immediately after the event; the other erected by public subscription in France, Luxemburg, and Bohemia in memory of those who fell in the battle.

Although the towns radiating from the village of Visnes-auval (occupied by the Battalion) were rather bare in these months of winter, their historical associations lent color to them, making them interesting and attractive.

Christmas had come round once again—the third Christmas they spent in France, and happily the last.

The weather had been boisterous and wet, but on Christmas morning the sun shone out to brighten one of the happiest days spent in France. Company dinners were held in the roomy billets, where at 1 o'clock the Battalion cooks served a sumptuous meal, which received an ovation.

Lieut.-Colonel Hurry, D.S.O., the unit's popular commander, visited the happy companies as they sat at dinner to wish them a Merry Christmas, and to receive a warm welcome.

Once again the 10th Brigade Comforts Fund had given Father Christmas a commission, for on Christmas Eve every member of the Battalion received an "Aussie parcel" packed and despatched by the untiring hands of the Comforts Fund workers in far-away Victoria. Each parcel contained the Season's Greetings and a message of good cheer. Everyone realised what a wonderful work was being done for their comfort by the senders of the parcels. It was not only at Christmas time that this was realised, for regular supplies of comforts were continually arriving from Australia, and the "Thank you" that escaped the lips of the recipients of the good things were the expressions of truly grateful hearts.

Leave to Abbeville and the surrounding towns was granted in the afternoon, when the perfect weather added to the day's enjoyment.

The fighting being over, the training now carried out was of a very mild nature, and really amounted to daily exercise so necessary to ensure the physical fitness of so many men. Easy route marches became very popular, for it was no pleasure to be idle in these days, flavored with Winter's sharp sting. Lectures and classes on educational subjects were held; but a matter of still greater interest was the filling in of Repatriation Forms. The word DEMOBILISATION constantly figured in daily conversations. There was something magical about this word. It spelt **AUSTRALIA** in large, glowing letters. It led one's thoughts to sunny shores, and on into the vast bushlands, and into the bright glow of the home fireside.

Men were restless nowadays, restless for a sight of the homeland. This was natural, but wise heads had fashioned weapons to combat this feeling of restlessness. Educational classes, lectures, sports meetings, concerts and dances fought it, and almost conquered it. Although the call of the Homeland still rang in men's ears, there were times when it subsided to a whisper. The voices of English girls hushed it, merry-faced girls, who came along in their neat khaki costumes to dance with the "Digger," and cheer the hours of waiting.

And so the days at Vismes-au-val were full of interest, and if any man found them dull he had but himself to blame.

At last the day arrived (Monday, 17th February) when the first draft from the 38th Battalion left the peaceful little village en route for Australia, via Le Havre and England. With light hearts and eager footsteps 14 officers, 36 N.C.O's., and 257 men stepped out on to the homeward track.

"The Long, Long Trail," which had wound for so long a time through dangerous and difficult ways, was now growing short, and led through the sunshine of peace and happiness.

Many had fallen where the trail led through "The Valley of the Shadow," and those who now marched away remembered them, and cherished their memory.

And they, and those who were soon to follow, were to carry back to their native land an imperishable record of Honor and Glory.

One of their proud boasts was that only five (5) members of the Battalion had been captured by the enemy, and the capture of these men brought no shame upon the Unit, for four had been badly wounded, and the fifth lost in the darkness of "No Man's Land," to unconsciously wander into the enemy territory.

And so the first draft to return to Australia marched down the sunlit Trail to the strains of the Old Battalion Band as Morning came to meet them over the hills of Picardy.

THE END.

: Appendix :

ROLL OF HONORS.

DISTINGUISHED SERVICE ORDER.
Lieutenant-Colonel Davis, C. H., 5/6/17.
Major Hurry, G., 4-12/10/17, Ypres.
Captain Davies, G. V., 4-12/10/17, Ypres.

THE MILITARY CROSS.
2nd Lieut. Emonson, K. G., 16/12/16, Houplines.
Lieut. Peters, C. H., 2/1/17, Houplines.
,, McCulloch, W. H., 28/5/17, Ploegsteert Raid.
,, Kennedy, T. H., 28/5/17, Ploegsteert Raid.
Capt. Fairweather, F. E., 7-9/6/17, Messines.
,, Trebilcock, R. E., 7-9/6/17, Messines.
,, Fraser, A., 7-9/6/17, Messines.
,, Latchford, E. W. 12/10/18, Ypres.
,, Orchard, W. H., 4/10/18, Ypres.
Lieut. Martin, F. R. B., 4/10/18, Ypres.
2nd Lieut. Schlitz, E. J. H., 10/2/18, Warneton Raid.
,, Churchill, J. A. B., 10/2/18, Warneton Raid.
Lieut. Baxter, F. J., 19/10/18, Ypres.
,, Sandiford, N. W. W., 28/8/18, Curlu.
,, Eason, J. F., 29/8/18, Clery.
,, Telfer, P. J., 4/11/18, Bony.
,, Robbins, H., 31/8/18, Clery.
,, Crispe, C. T., 31/8/18, Clery.

BAR TO MILITARY CROSS.
Capt. Fairweather, F. E., 28/5/18, Marett Wood.
Lieut. Baxter, F. J., 28/10/18, Clery.
Capt. Peters, C. H., 4/11/18, Bony.

DISTINGUISHED CONDUCT MEDAL.
Sgt. Taylor, A. J. C., 28/2/18, Armentieres Raid.
Pte. Lock, F., 28/5/17, Ploegsteert Raid.
Sgt. Nihill, P. L., 7-9/6/17, Messines.
Cpl. Fullerton, G. B., 7-9/6/17, Messines.
L.-Cpl. Perry, F. J., Continuous record of good work as Scout.
L.-Cpl. Bright, A. A. G., 4/10/17, Ypres.
Sgt. Shilliday, J. S., 4/10/17, Ypres.
Sgt. Heaney, J. R., 29/8/18, Clery.
Cpl. Grinton, A. V., 28/8/18, Curlu.

MERITORIOUS SERVICE MEDAL.
Sgt. Mulquinny, E.   L.-Cpl. McDonald, J. A.

THE MILITARY MEDAL.

Pte. Meyerink, J. J., 16/12/16, Houplines.
Cpl. Nihill, P. L., 28/2/17, Armentieres Raid.
Pte. Tutor, H. W. H., 28/2/17. Armentieres Raid.
„ Shuttlewood, J. A., 28/2/17, Armentieres Raid.
„ McIvor, P., 28/2/17, Armentieres Raid.
„ Green T. A., 7-9/6/17, Messines.
L.-Sgt. Berry, R. P., 7-9/6/17, Messines.
Pte. Moore, A. S., 7-9/6/17, Messines.
„ Coutts, P. R., 7-9/6/17, Messines.
„ Pyers, L., 7-9/6/17, Messines.
Cpl. Spencer, G., 7-9/6/17, Messines.
Pte. Holt, G., 7-9/6/17, Messines.
„ Pascoe, J. T., 7-9/6/17, Messines.
„ Joiner, W. E., 7-9/6/17, Messines.
„ Eyers, A. L., 7-9/6/17, Messines.
„ Heaney, J. R., 7-9/6/17, Messines.
Sgt. Buckland, R. J. 7-9/6/17, Messines.
Cpl. Roberts, L. A., 7-9/6/17, Messines.
T.-Sgt. Brook, W. F., 4-5/10/17, Ypres.
Pte. Petherick, A. V., 4-5/10/17, Ypres.
„ Chalmers, T. M., 4-5/10/17, Ypres.
Cpl. Crafter, F. S. H., 4-5/10/17, Ypres.
Pte. Stanbury, W. E., 4-5/10/17, Ypres.
„ Seymour, C. E., 4-5/10/17, Ypres.
„ Smith, L. C., 4-5/10/17, Ypres.
Sgt. Siden, O. H., 4-5/10/17, Ypres.
Pte. Guthridge, J. G., 4-5/10/17, Ypres.
„ Chalmers, P., 4-5/10/17, Ypres.
„ McMaster, E., 4-5/10/17, Ypres.
Cpl. White, H. B., 4-5/10/17, Ypres.
Pte. Tranter, B. A., 4-5/10/17, Ypres.
Sgt. Fraser, H. J., 4-12/10/17, Ypres.
„ King, J. H. S., 4-12/10/17, Ypres.
Cpl. Meredith, J. V., 4-12/10/17, Ypres.
L.-Cpl. Campbell, G., 4-12/10/17, Ypres.
Sgt. Beard, E. S., 4-12/10/17, Ypres.
„ Burke, J., 4-12/10/17, Ypres.
Pte. Fedder, F., 4-12/10/17, Ypres.
„ Matheson, J., 4-12/10/17, Ypres.
Cpl. Bell, I. L., 4-12/10/17, Ypres.
Pte. Hollingworth. A., 4-12/10/17, Ypres.
„ Gelly, R. M. L., 10/2/18, Warneton Raid.
Cpl. Wallace, J., 10/2/18, Warneton Raid.
Pte. Grant. J., 10/2/18, Warneton Raid.
„ Umbers, E. C., 10/2/18, Warneton Raid.
L.-Cpl. Dunn. —J. N. W. E., 10/2/18, **Warneton Raid.**
Pte. Cheek, C. H., 10/2/18, Warneton Raid.
„ Rowe, P. B., 10/2/18, Warneton Raid.
L.-Cpl. McDonald, J. R., 10/2/18, **Warneton Raid.**
Pte. Nihill, J. J., 10/2/18, Warneton Raid.
„ Price, G. F., 11/8/18, Proyart.
„ Allitt, J. W. H., 11/8/18/, Proyart.
„ Smith, E. A. G., 11/8/18, Proyart.
L.-Cpl. Lewis, J. C., 11/8/18, Proyart.
Pte. Taylor, P. H., 11/8/18, Proyart.
„ **Williams,** T. G., 11/8/18, Proyart.
L.-Cpl. Newell, W. J. L., 4 12/10/17, Ypres.

Cpl. Pegler, A. E., 29/8/18, Curlu—Clery.
Sgt. Baum, H. A., 29/8/18, Curlu—Clery.
Pte. Todd, A. J., 29/8/18, Curlu—Clery.
„ Stevens, H. J. 29/8/18, Curlu—Clery.
„ McCoy, F. C., 29/8/18, Curlu—Clery.
Cpl. Newton, C. E., Curlu—Clery.
L.-Cpl. De La Ray, F. J., 29/8/18, Curlu—Clery.
Pte. Amiet, H., 29/8/18, Curlu—Clery.
„ Purcell, G. V., 29/8/18, Curlu—Clery.
Sgt. Raybould, A. J. B., 1/10/18, Bony.
Cpl. Paton, R. W., 1/10/18, Bony.
Pte. McPherson, A., 1/10/18, Bony.
„ Hedgecock, E. E., 1/10/18, Bony.
„ Shillinglaw, E. S., 1/10/18, Bony.
L.-Cpl. Cookson, W. W., 1/10/18, Bony.
Pte. Haythorne, A. B., 1/10/18, Bony.
„ McMaster, A., 1/10/18, Bony.
Sgt. Lehman, F. W., 1/10/18, Bony.
T.-Cpl. Nicholson, H., Peace Despatch, Messines, and other actions.

BAR TO MILITARY MEDAL.

Sgt. Beard, E. S., 1/10/18, Bony.
Sgt. Meredith, J. V.

CROIX DE GUERRE.

Pte. Sinclair, R. B., Ypres.
Sgt. Branch, R. B. B., Ypres.
Cpl. Raybould, A. T. B., Warneton Raid.
Pte. Hollingworth, H., Continuous record of good work.
L.-Cpl. Landells, A. W., Continuous record of good work.
Pte. Luke, J. H., Continuous record of good work.

MENTIONED IN DESPATCHES.

Lieut.-Col. Davis, C. H., 5/6/17.
Capt. Marks, R. M., 5/6/17.
„ Fraser, A., 5/6/17.
Lieut. Gale, C. C., 5/6/17.
Cpl. Murphy, T. G., 8/6/17.
Capt. Dench, H., 30/12/17.
Lieut. Langley, F. B., 30/12/17.
Cpl. Pegler, A. E., 30/12/17.
Pte. Nicholson, H., 30/12/17.
Lieut.-Col. Davis, C. H., D.S.O., V.D., 28/5/17.
Major Hurry, G., D.S.O., 28/5/18.
„ Maudsley, A. J. A., 28/5/18.
Lieut. O'Donnell, J. B., 28/5/18.
L.-Cpl. Lewis, J. C., 28/5/18.
R.Q.M.S. Nicholl, J. W. A., 28/5/18.
Capt. Dench, H., 1/1/19.
Lt. Major, E. W. H. 1/1/19.
Sgt. Marrett, F. W. P., 1/1/19.
Capt. Beattie, L. J., 11/7/19.

MEN WHO SERVED WITH THE BATTALION.

OFFICERS.

Asterisk (✸) denotes "The Supreme Sacrifice."

Lieut. Angus, J. N.
    ,, Addison, D. Mc G.
Capt. Akeroyd, J. A.
✸Lieut. Abbey, E. G.
    ,, Baxter, F. J.
    ,, Bogle, W. L.
    ,, Bennett, W. F.
    ,, Bowden, H. H.
Capt. Beattie, L. J.
Chaplain Brown, C. P.
Lieut. Bult, R. B.
    ,, Bowman, G. G.
    ,, Barker, E. M.
    ,, Birchell, L. J.
✸,, Blair, T. H.
    ,, Baum, H. A.
    ,, Crispe, C. T.
✸,, Callan, C. J.
    ,, Crisfield, H.
Capt. Collins, W. J.
✸Lieut. Cadusch, J. J.
    ,, Cloke, F. J.
    ,, Churchill, J. A. B.
    ,, Coutts, P.
✸Capt. Dench, H.
    ,, Davies, G. V.
Colonel Davis, C. H.
Lieut. Davis, J. C.
    ,, Duigan, G. L.
    ,, Dunn, T. H.
✸,, Dutton, G. A.
2nd Lieut. Emmonson, K. G.
Lieut. Eason, J. F.
Chaplain Esperson, O. C.
Lieut. Fitzgerald, G. E.
    ,, Fenner, N. W.
Capt. Fraser, A.
✸,, Fairweather, F. E.
Lieut. Fairweather, H. A.
Lieut. Fleming, J. A.
Chaplain Freer, D. L.
Lieut. Gollan, R. W.
    ,, Gale, C. C.
Chaplain Gunson, W. N.
✸Major Henderson, R. O.
Lieut. Herring, P. C.
    ,, Heward, F. L.
Lt.-Col. Hurry, G.
Chaplain Heyden, H. A.
Lieut. Holmberg, J.
✸,, Hyett, A. N.
    ,, Hutchins, G. L.

✸Lieut. Killingsworth, H. L.
✸,, Kennedy, T. H.
✸,, Kirkbride, R.
    ,, Langley, F.B.
Capt. Lansell, G. V.
    ,, Latchford, E. W.
Lieut. Lipshutt, L.
    ,, Munday, J. J.
    ,, Marquis, S. C.
    ,, Major, E. W. H.
✸,, Morrison, F. C.
    ,, Martin, F. R. B.
Capt. Marks, R. M.
✸Lieut. Matthews, C.
✸Capt. Moore, E. F.
    ,, Moore, J. H.
Lieut. Murie, W. P. D.
✸,, Maxwell, W.
    ,, Macoboy, F. F.
✸,, Marshall, K. E. D.
✸Major Maudsley, A. J. A.
Lieut. Malloch, P.
    ,, Mills, G.
    ,, Marlow, A. S.
    ,, Mitchell, L. W.
Capt. Mailer, M. H.
    ,, Marshall, T. E.
    ,, Metcalfe, J.
✸Lieut. McColl, H.
    ,, Mackay, F. I.
    ,, McPherson, C. S.
✸,, McKenzie, D.
    ,, McCulloch, W. H.
Capt. McCusker, J.
    ,, McPhee, R.
    ,, Orchard, W. H.
Lieut. O'Donnell, J. B.
    ,, O'Collins, F. J.
Major Pollard, L. L.
Lieut. Poole, H. F.
✸,, Pooley, J. E.
    ,, Potter, E.
    ,, Phillips, T. P.
Capt. Peters, C. H.
Lieut. Robb, L. S.
    ,, Rooke, T. A. R.
    ,, Robbins, H.
✸,, Riddell, R. B.
✸,, Robinson, T. C.
    ,, Rowe, W. L.
    ,, Reid, A. H.
    ,, Roberts, L. A.

Lieut. Storey, E.
Lieut. Spedding, Q. S.
✥Capt. Selleck, H. F.
Lieut. Spark, P. S.
 „ Schlitz, E. J. H.
Capt. Sweeney.
Lieut. Shilliday, J. S.
Capt. Solling.
 „ Smith, L. L.
Lieut. Sandiford, N. W. W.
Lieut. Telfer, P. J.
Capt. Trebilcock, R. E.

✥Lieut. Thomas, H.
✥ „ Thompson, W. T.
Capt. Tyers, R. W.
Lieut. Verso, S. B.
 „ Williams, W.
 „ Wilson, W. G.
 „ Warnock, S. R.
 „ Wardale-Greenwood, H.
✥ „ Wyndham, H. S.
✥ „ Watson, C. A.
 „ Whitehead, J. L.

✤ ✤ ✤ ✤

OFFICERS WHO JOINED FROM OTHER BATTALIONS.

Lieut. Aitken, P. L., 37th Battalion.
 „ Bool, A. L., 37th Battalion.
 „ Boyland, W. J., 37th Battalion.
 „ Crowe, W. H. W. 37th Battalion.
 „ Chalmers, L. A., 37th Battalion.
Capt. Cooper, F. H. W., 37th Battalion.
Lieut. Dorrington, I. A., 37th Battalion.
2nd Lieut. Ellis, A. R., 39th Battalion.
Major Hutton, C. R., 39th Battalion.
Capt. Heberle, F. C., 37th Battalion.
Lieut. Isherwood, P. L., 37th Battalion.
2nd Lieut. Jamieson, E. A., 39th Battalion.
 „ „ Low, J. S., 37th Battalion.
Lieut. Meader, T. A., 37th Battalion.
 „ Murdoch, A. M., 37th Battalion.
2nd Lieut. McEwan, J. F., 39th Battalion.
Lieut. McNicol, N. G., 37th Battalion.
 „ O'Malley, W. B., 37th Battalion.
 „ Partridge, R. L., 37th Battalion.
Lieut. Robertson, L. J., 37th Battalion.
 „ Rennick, F. S., 37th Battalion.
Major Robertson, W. F. H., 37th Battalion.
2nd Lieut. Robinson, G. H., 9th F. Amb.
Lieut. Smith, A. W., 37th Battalion.
 „ Smith, R. J., 37th Battalion.
 „ Stewart, A., 37th Battalion.
 „ Stokes, M. R., 37th Battalion.
 „ Spalding, J. A., 37th Battalion.
 „ Tully, J. H., 3rd Div. Train.
 „ Wood, E. D., 37th Battalion.
2nd Lieut. Collard, R., 10th M.G. Company.
Lieut. Watkins.

OTHER RANKS.

Sgt. Adam, R. H.
„ Adams, J. E.
Pte. Aitken, J. R.
„ Adwin. W. J.
✣ „ Ainsworth, P. T.
„ Allen, A. T.
„ Allen, T. F.
✣ ., Allen, R.
L.-Cpl. Alberd, R. D.
„ Allen, J.
✣Pte. Allen, T. P.
,. Allbutt, N.
„ Allitt, G. F.
„ Allitt, J. W. H.
„ Alexander, J.
„ Alexander, R. S.
„ Aldridge, E. J.
Cpl. Amiet, H.
Pte. Amato, E.
„ Alcock, H.
L.-Sgt. Amos, W. E. C.
Pte. Ambrose, H.
L.-Cpl. Ankatell. J. K.
Pte. Angwin. J.
„ Anderson, T. P. S.
L.-Cpl. Andrews, W. T.
Pte. Anderson, W.
„ Andrews, H. V.
„ Anderson. R. F.
„ Angwin, B. W.
.. Anson, E. J.
✣Cpl. Anderson, T.
✣Pte. Anderson, J. H.
Pte. Andrews, W. F. P.
„ Anderson, C. R.
✣ „ Andrew, A.
.. Appleby, C. E.
.. Argus, W.
„ Artis, A. E.
✣ .. Arthur, H. J.
✣ „ Arthur, G. A.
✣ „ Armstrong, W. J.
L.-Cpl. Archibald, H. J.
✣Pte. Archibald, E. C. W.
✣ „ Arthur, W. H.
„ Armitage, L.T.
✣ ., Arthur, L. G.
„ Armstrong, C. H.
„ Argles, J.
✣ „ Ashman, A. A.
„ Ash, S. R.
„ Ash, N. B.
„ Atkins, W. H.
✣ „ Aubrey, A. G.
„ Axford, F.

Pte. Bartlett, J. A. F.
.. Batt, W. E.
,. Ballenger, G. E.
✣,. Barclay, C. O.
✣ „ Barrow, F.
Dvr. Baldwin, W. J. C.
✣Pte. Barnden, C. J.
No. 512, Baker, J. R.
Pte. Backhouse, E.
L.-Cpl. Barker, L. F.
Pte. Baird, C. C.
„ Baldwin, E. C.
„ Batchelor, S.
„ Barry, C.
„ Barker, F.
„ Barr, C. M.
✣ „ Barry, G.
„ Bateman, W. J.
., Barclay, E. H.
„ Barling, H. J.
✣ „ Baker, E.
✣No. 467, Baker, J. R.
Pte. Bailey, J.
„ Batty, J. T.
„ Battley, E. A.
✣ ,. Bale, W. J.
.. Backman, F. G.
„ Baxter, T. J.
„ Bailey, H. R.
„ Barlow, M.
„ Bain, G.
Cpl. Barkell, C.
L.-Cpl. Barbour, R.
Pte. Ball, T.
✣ „ Bastian, A. R.
„ Baum, H. L.
„ Bateman, A.
„ Banks, C. H.
„ Barkas, A.
„ Barmby, W. H.
✣ ., Ball, R. W.
„ Barnett, E. A.
✣ „Bateman, S. A.
Cpl. Beilby, W. J.
✣Pte. Bellingham, S. M.
., Bennett, T. A.
„ Beardsall, T.
„ Beamish, R. S.
„ Bevan, R. H.
„ Bennett, T. J.
Sgt. Beard, E. S.
✣Pte. Begbie, A. H.
„ Bennett, H.
Cpl. Bellamy, R. L.
Pte. Beves, F. A.

HISTORY OF 38th BATTALION, A.I.F. 93

Pte. Bentley, L. C.
L.-Cpl. Berry, G. T.
Sgt. Berry, R. R.
Cpl. Bell, I. L.
Pte. Beatty, S.
✣Pte. Beaseley, W. J.
✣ „ Beasley, G. A.
„ Bell, R. W.
„ Berry, D.
„ Beasley, A.
„ Becker, E.
„ Bennett, C. J.
✣ ., „ Berry, G.
„ Benson, A. D.
.. Bell, A. W.
Sgt. Bedworth, J.
Pte. Beeton, G. H.
„ Bence, G. F.
,. Beesley, J.
.. Berry, D.
✣ ,. Beilby, J.
„ Beverley, E. P.
., Binion, F.
✣ „ Birdsall, J. G.
✣ ., Bird, F. L.
Sgt. Bilston, G.
Dvr. Birmingham, F. J.
L.Cpl Bird, E.
✣Pte. Bligh, F. J.
„ Blampied, R. J.
„ Black, L. L. G.
✣ ,. Bliss, F. H.
„ Blake, T. M.
✣ „ Blair, W. A.
., Black, S.
„ Blackburn, L. J.
„ Black, J. K.
✣ ,. Blaxall, K. E.
., Blake, W. W.
.. Bodger, T. J. H.
.. Boyd, J.
✣ „ Boyling, G. M.
✣ „ Bond, G. R.
✣ ,. Booth, H.
., Boyle, A.
✣L.-Cpl. Boyd, R. S.
Pte. Boyle, D. L.
.. Booth, R. A.
✣Dvr. Box, H. R.
Pte. Bowles, T.
„ Boyd, E. J.
„ Bosenberg, F. R.
„ Boyle, N. C.
„ Boak, P. J.
„ Boyd, A. H.
„ Booth, C. B.
„ Bolt, L. A.

Pte. Bonham, R. L.
„ Bowen, W.
✣L.-Cpl. Boorman, C. H.
✣Sgt. Bourke, J.
Pte. Bourke, J. J.
✣A.-Sgt. Bowen, J. H.
✣Cpl. Bone, P. J.
Pte. Bond, F. E.
„ Booth, T. H.
,. Bowman, W. W.
„ Bright, E. J.
„ Branigan, C. J.
✣ ., Brotherton, R. B.
L.-Sgt. Brook, W. F.
Sgt. Breen, L. T.
✣Pte. Brown, R. P.
„ Brasier, W. M.
Cpl. Brookes, A. E.
Pte. Brown, C.
„ Bridges, A.
„ Brown, J. E.
„ Brown, R. S.
„ Bryer-Jones, G. R.
, Brotherton, H. W. P.
„ Brown, H.
„ Brown, L. A.
✣ ., Brant, H.
✣ „ Brown, J.
Sgt. Branch, R. B.
Pte. Bridgeman, S. T.
„ Brown, J. C.
„ Bray, A. J.
„ Bray, R. E.
✣ ., Bright, C.
✣ ., Britton, J. N.
✣ „ Braid, W.
„ Bray, R. H.
„ Braddy, W.
Sgt. Brockhouse, E. H.
Pte. Brown, S. J.
„ Bridle, N.
.. Brown, C.
Sgt. Brown, A. S.
✣Pte. Brotherton, W. L.
„ Brodie, J. W.
„ Bromley, G.
„ Brown, H. W.
„ Broadbent, J. E.
Dvr. Brown, H.
Pte. Brown, J. J.
„ Brotherton, C.
„ Brown, C. H.
Cpl. Bruce, E. N.
Pte. Brady, V.
✣ ., Bradfield, W.
„ Bright, A. A. G.
„ Brellin, J. B.

Pte. Bradshaw, A. N.
Cpl. Brodie. C. S. M
Pte. Butler, E.
L.-Cpl. Briant, R. W. V.
Pte. Brereton, E. H.
„ Brennan, J. J.
„ Burns, A. E.
Cpl. Bullen, J.
Pte. Burlock, H. W.
„ Butt, O. B.
„ Bull, P. R.
C.S.M. Buckland, T. M.
„ Buckland, R. J.
✣Pte Buckley, E. A.
„ Bull, H. F.
✣Sgt. Burke, J.
L.-Cpl. Bullen, D. M.
✣Pte. Burt, T. C.
„ Burgess, C. K.
„ Burton, H. O.
„ Burgdorf, H. C.
Sgt. Burroughs, E. C.
Pte. Burtenshaw, R.
„ Bulman, B.
„ Bullen, R. W.
L.-Cpl. Buckley, C. S.
Pte. Burgess, G. F.
„ Byrnes, J.
„ Byron, A. T.
✣„ Byrne, V. B.
„ Byrnes, P.
„ Campbell, R. W.
„ Campbell, L. W.
✣„ Cansick, P. J. F.
„ Carey, A. J. R.
„ Canty, J. L.
„ Cardoza, J. R.
„ Cahill, V M.
„ Cameron, A. M.
„ Cameron, J.
„ Cameron, S. A.
„ Carter, J. L.
„ Cafferty, E. J.
✣„ Camp, W. J.
„ Cameron, E. A.
✣„ Casey, J.
„ Carr, A. F. J.
„ Campbell, A.
„ Callaghan, T. M.
„ Carse, H. C. S.
„ Cayless, R. G. J.
✣„ Carter, P.
„ Carney, P. V.
✣„ Callen, J. D.
„ Carter, W. T.
„ Cana, C. C.
„ Carlson, I.

Pte. Carss, H. C. S.
„ Cardwell, F. E.
„ Capp, R. W.
Cpl. Cayless, R. G. J.
Pte. Cassidy, R. A. G.
✣„ Carr, G. A.
„ Canny, J. A.
„ Cant, W. L. H.
Sgt. Cassidy, W. H.
✣Pte. Cameron, A. E.
„ Caldwell, H. R. A.
„ Campbell, G. L.
„ Capner, E. E.
Cpl. Campbell, G.
„ Cann, F. C.
Pte. Card, A. J.
„ Cain, J.
„ Cameron, J.
„ Cecil, D. A.
✣„ Champion, J.
„ Cheek, C. H.
„ Chalmers, A. G.
✣„ Chalmers, P.
„ Chalmers, T. M.
„ Chenoweth, G. R.
„ Challis, A. E.
✣„ Chapman, C. V.
„ Christie, H. D.
Sgt. Chambers, A. E.
Pte. Chivers, J. H.
„ Cherry, H.
Sgt. Chittock, A. W. L.
Pte. Chamberlain, W. A.
L.-Cpl. Chisholm, A.
Pte. Cliff, A. H.
„ Clifford, B. G.
✣„ Clark, W. T.
„ Clarke, H. C.
„ Clothier, J. G.
„ Clark, E. G.
„ Clarke, H. C.
„ Cluley, G. W.
„ Clayton, W. J.
„ Clark, J. E.
„ Clarke, W. R.
✣„ Cleary, T.
„ Clarke, J. R.
„ Clack, S.
L.-Cpl. Clancy, D.
Pte. Clifton, L. B. W.
L.-Sgt. Clarke, F. L.
Pte. Clarke, G.
„ Clarke, A. H.
✣„ Clarke, F. E.
„ Clarke, N. O.
„ Cleaver, L. G. E.
Cpl. Clark, A. L.

HISTORY OF 38th BATTALION, A.I.F.   95

Cpl. Clarke, C. H.
Drv. Clarke, A. W. S. N.
✤Pte. Clinnick, G. A. S.
,, Cloke, J. B.
,, Clutterbuck, W. P.
,, Clarke, R. H.
,, Clare, S.
C.S.M. Clark, A.
L.-Cpl. Cookson, W.W.
Pte. Coughlin, M. J.
,, Coram, A. A.
✤,, Collins, T. W.
L.-Cpl. Courtney, P.
Pte. Cowley, R. T.
,, Code, A. M.
,, Conley, R. K.
L.-Cpl. Corkhill, C. A.
Sgt. Code, J. J.
L.-Cpl. Coleman, M. G. D.
Pte. Cogan, J.
,, Cooke, A.
,, Cowan, J.
,, Cousins, R. S.
,, Cozens, W. T.
,, Cornell, C. S.
✤,, Coghill, J. A.
✤,, Cook, W. T.
L.-Cpl. Cork, W. J.
Pte. Code, E. T.
,, Cooper, C.
✤,, Collins, T. J.
Cpl. Cox, S. I.
✤Pte. Coulson, R. G.
✤,, Collins, C. C. C.
,, Cooper, A. A.
✤,, Costa, T.
,, Collins, T. C.
,, Corbett, W. L.
,, Cox, E. V.
,, Collison, G. H.
,, Cowper, J. E.
,, Connolly, A. H.
,, Cochrane, C. T.
,, Cole, R. J.
Sgt. Coffey, J.
Pte. Cochrane, W. W.
Sgt. Codling, H.
Pte. Collins, G. C.
,, Condick, J. A.
Sgt. Cook, F. G.
✤Pte. Costello, R.
,, Constable, W. M.
,, Coffey, B. J.
✤Sgt. Coutts, T. A.
Pte. Cockayne, G.
✤,, Conlon, B. J.
,, Cooper, A. L.

Pte. Connelly, M. J.
,, Cooper, J. J.
,, Cole, T. H.
,, Cooper, R.
,, Cooke, H.
✤,, Cooper, J. C.
,, Coulson, O. J.
,, Crellin, J. B.
,, Crosby, H.
,, Crosby, R.
,, Crawford, F. R.
,, Critch, J. J.
✤,, Cranston, J. T.
,, Crafter, F. S. H.
,, Crockett, A. H.
,, Crowder, A. H.
,, Craig, G. E.
✤,, Cross, H. B.
L.-Cpl. Crook, J. R.
✤Pte. Crookes, F.
,, Cutting, R.
,, Cummings, E. W.
,, Cush, W. L.
✤,, Cumming, W. J.
,, Cummin, A. N.
,, Curran, F. A.
,, Cunningham, T. J.
,, Cullinan, J. T.
,, Cuttriss, J.
✤S.-Sgt. Cunningham, P. J.
Pte. Currie, J.
,, Cull, J. B.
✤,, Curle, O.
✤,, Davies, A. G.
Dvr. Davis, H. V.
Pte. Daniel, S. D.
,, Darcy, G. E.
,, Davidson, R.
,, Dalton, J. C.
,, Dalli, J.
✤,, Dalzell, C.
,, Davis, R. G.
,, Dare, G.
,, Davenport, C. G.
,, Dalrymple, E. J.
,, Dalton, A. E.
,, Davidge, C.
,, Davis, E. W.
,, Davis, A. F.
✤,, Dawtrey, S. G.
Sgt. Dalgleish, A. S.
✤Pte. Daish, F.
✤,, Day, S. F.
✤,, Day, W. J.
,, Davies, E. F. B.
,, Darnley, A.
✤,, Davenport, A. V.

HISTORY OF 38th BATTALION, A.I.F.

Pte. Davies, A. R.
Cpl. Dabb, H. T. S.
Pte. Dart, R.
„ Davis, W.
„ Davenport, C. G.
„ Davidson, N. G.
„ Delaney, T. E.
„ Dervan, W. L.
„ Deans, H.
„ Dennis, G. T.
„ Dee, F. M.
„ De Leon, C. A.
Cpl. Deal, F. S.
Pte. Delahoy, G. O.
✢L.-Cpl. Delaney, J.
✢L.-Cpl. De la Ray, F. J.
✢Pte. Dewar, W.
„ Dearricott, C. A.
„ Delbridge, J.
„ De Carle, C. J.
✢„ D'Araugo, F.
„ Dewing, H. R.
„ Dinsdale, E.
✢„ Dickenson, R.
„ Dickenson, N.
„ Dickman, F. E.
„ Dickinson, T. W.
„ Dickson, C. C.
„ Dickenson, T. H.
„ Dickenson, H. J.
Cpl. Dick, H. G.
Pte. Diggle, J. L.
„ Diergarden, W. F.
✢„ Downing, H.
✢„ Doherty, R.
„ Doyle, J.
✢„ Donovan, T.
„ Donovan, S. G.
„ Down, H. C.
„ Doyle, J. T.
„ Dodds, F.
✢„ Doyle, I. R.
„ Douglas, T. M.
„ Donaldson, B. M.
„ Dorr, C. A.
Sgt. Donovan, H. A.
Cpl. Downes, P. C.
Pte. Donald, H. G.
„ Donald, A. J.
„ Downing, H. O.
✢„ Dower, A. E.
✢„ Doherty, J. G.
„ Dolan, J. F. J.
„ Dodd, W.
✢„ Dohle, E.
„ Dole, M. W.
„ Doyle, P.

Pte. Drummond, A_{1}. P. H.
✢„ Drever, J.
„ Drury, R. S.
✢„ Dryden, H. T.
L.-Cpl. Dunn, J. N. W. E.
Pte. Dunn, A. W.
„ Dunn, V. H. L.
✢„ Duff, R. W.
✢„ Dunn, C. E. A.
C.S.M. Durward, W. J.
✢Cpl. Dutton, A. E
Pte. Duke, G. S.
„ Dunn, P. G.
Sgt. Dunn, G.
„ Duffy, C. J. A.
✢L.-Cpl. Duke, F.
L.-Cpl. Duncan, A.
„ Durham, G. H.
„ Du Bois, E.
„ Dunkerly, J. H.
„ Duplantier, H. E.
Pte. Duggan, T.
„ Duffy, E. G.
L.-Cpl. Dyer, W. C.
Pte. Eaton, R. O.
„ Easton, A.
„ Earl, A. W.
Dvr. Easton, F. J.
✢Pte. Eckford, P. W.
Pte. Eddy, R.
„ Edwards, C.
„ Edwards, O.
L.-Cpl. Edwards, H. R.
Pte. Eddington, S. J.
„ Eddy, H. M.
„ Edmonds, R. S. T.
„ Edwards, C.
„ Edwards, C. F.
„ Eddlebuttle, J.
„ Edwards, H.
✢„ Edmonds, W. A
„ Eddy, W. B.
„ Egan, W.
✢„ Eldridge, W. R.
R.S.M. Elliott, G. M.
✢Pte. Ellis, A. J.
✢„ Ellis, W.
„ Elliott, S. J.
„ Elliott, F.
„ Elston, L.
✢„ Eldridge, J.
„ Elliott, S. V.
„ Elliott, A. A.
„ Entwistle, J. J.
„ Engstrom, G. I. A.
„ Ennis, F. E.
✢„ Erickson, W. F.

HISTORY OF 38th BATTALION, A.I.F. 97

✢Cpl. Ethell, F.
Pte. Evans, K.
" Evans, J. P.
" Evans, R. A.
" Evans, R. D.
Dvr. Exon, G. E.
Pte. Exelby, W. T.
" Eyers, A. L.
" Fasso, M. A.
" Farrel, W. A.
" Falting, W. A. B.
✢ " Falconbridge, W.
" Fauvel, P. H.
" Fasham, A. C.
" Fairey, E.
,. Fawcett, H.
" Farrell, T. A.
" Farnell, J. T.
" Fenton, C. W.
" Ferguson, J. M.
" Ferguson, C. A.
✢ " Fewell, A.
" Ferguson, G. E.
" Ferguson, G.
" Feldman, F. A.
" Fennessy, J.
Cpl. Feder, F.
Pte. Fiddock, A. T.
" Findlay, C. T.
Sgt. Fiven, J. E.
✢Pte. Fisher, E.
" Fisk, H. W.
" Fielding, W. J.
" Fisher, A. N.
" Fisher, G. E. C.
" Fitzmaurice, W. H.
✢ " Fisher, W. D.
✢ " Finlay, H. J.
L.-Cpl. Finlayson, M.
Pte. Finnegan, M. A.
., Fisher, F. W.
" Flahive, W.
L.-Cpl. Fleigner, H. A.
Pte. Flowers, H. J.
" Flaherty, M. J.
" Fletcher, J.
✢.," Fleming, M.
✢L.-Cpl. Flack, P.
Pte. Fox, A. H.
✢ " Forrister, J. P.
C.Q.M.S. Fowler, W. L.
✢Pte. Fox, M. C.
" Fowler, C. J.
" Fowler, H.
" Foster, A.
" Forrest, F. G.
L.-Cpl. Fowler, G. T.

Pte. Forster, W. C.
✢ " Forbes, J.
✢ " Fox, S. D.
" Forbes, G. M.
Cpl. Foster, M. J.
Pte. Foran, C.
" Frith, A. J.
" Frearson, A.
✢ " Freeman, G. A.
" Francis, S.
,. . Frost, R. N.
" Franklin, C.
Sgt. Freeman, N. B.
✢Pte. Franklin, E. J. L.
" Fraser, M. J.
✢ " Fry, W. A.
✢Sgt. Fraser, H. J.
✢Pte. Franks, R.
L.-Cpl. Fullerton, J. A.
✢Cpl. Fullerton, G. B.
Pte. Fulton, H.
✢ " Fyfe, A. E.
" Garnett, S. W. W.
" Gallpin, E. F.
" Gaynor, J. P. ✱
., Galbraith, J.
" Garratt, H. G.
✢ " Gardner, R. A.
✢ " Gardner, J. R.
" Galvin, T. H.
L.-Cpl. Garton, F. W.
Pte. Garlepp, G.
" Garnham, W. R.
" Gardner, G. H.
" Garton, C. H.
" Gartside, W. B.
✢ " Garner, S. H.
Cpl. Gaulton, J. E.
✢Pte. Gardner, M.
" George, W. F.
., Gent, H.
" Gelly, R. L. M.
" Gee, S. A.
" Geddes, W.
✢Dvr. Gilmour, J. T.
✢Pte. Gilhooley, A.
✢ " Gibaud, W. E.
" Gibson, W. H.
L.-Cpl. Gillespie, R.
✢Pte. Gibson, G. H.
" Giddens, J. J.
" Gidley, A. V.
" Gillham, W. R.
Dvr. Gillespie, C.
✢Pte. Gibson, G. F.
Pte. Gibbs, E. E.
✢ " Gibbons, V. N.

Pte. Giddens, J. J.
  „ Gill, H.
  „ Gilbert, P.
  „ Glennon, W.
  „ Glen, W. E.
Sgt. Gooding, C. R. E.
Pte. Good, C. L.
✣Pte. Goldsmith, E. G.
✣ „ Gould, T. J.
  „ Goodwin, A. L.
  „ Goulter, H.
  „ Gould, C. M. R.
  „ Greenwood, W. H.
✣L.-Cpl. Grimshaw, G.
Pte. Grant, J. L.
Sgt. Grinton, J. W.
✣Pte. Graham, A. G.
  „ Graham, R.
✣ „ Greenwood, A. L. M.
  „ Grant, J.
✣ „ Grigg, T.
  „ Grinter, V. R.
  „ Grey, A. T.
  „ Gray, G. C.
✣ „ Green, O. J.
  „ Grigg, H. J.
  „ Greenough, C. A.
  „ Grant, T. H. Mc.
  „ Granrott, L. G. J.
  „ Green, T. A.
  „ Greenwood, A. C.
  „ Gray, O. F.
  „ Gregory, A. J.
  „ Gross, G. F.
  „ Graham, G. D.
Sgt. Grinton, A. V.
✣Sgt. Graham, N.
  „ Griffiths, F. J.
  „ Grover, G. S.
Cpl. Grant, G.
Pte. Graham, L. F.
✣ „ Gunning, W. J.
Cpl. Guy, C.
Pte. Gunn, A. G.
  „ Guthridge, G. J.
L.-Cpl. Gunstan, J. F.
Pte. Gunnell, D. H. V.
Sgt. Guy, J. W.
Pte. Gunn, W. P.
L.-Sgt. Gudgeon, J. L. W.
✣Pte. Hall, F.
  „ Haywood, W. J.
  „ Hawke, H. H.
  „ Hamilton, V. S.
✣ „ Hancock, A. J. B.
  „ Hart, H. J.
Cpl. Harbourd, N. V.

L.-Cpl. Harbourd, L. W.
Pte. Hamilton, T. P.
  „ Hartley, W.
  „ Harwood, J.
  „ Hamilton, O. R.
✣ „ Harnell, H.
✣ „ Harder, W. J. C.
✣ „ Hales, E. H. L.
  „ Haupt, O. A.
  „ Hayes, E. A. L.
  „ Hardidge, A.
  „ Harris, A.
  „ Harris, R.
✣ „ Hart, W. M.
  „ Haythorne, A. B.
Sgt. Hayman, A.
Pte. Harris, T. J.
  „ Hardwick, A.
  „ Hanlon, J. J.
  „ Hayllar, H.
✣ „ Harding, C. C.
✣ „ Hawken, F. W.
L.-Cpl. Harris, E. J.
Pte. Hall, A. T.
  „ Halkett, C.
  „ Harris, H. G.
  „ Hall, V. J.
Cpl. Hall, C. E.
Pte. Hamilton, A. L.
  „ Hawken, H. S.
  „ Haynes, W. J.
  „ Hagan, T.
  „ Haynes, H. T.
✣ „ Hargrave, A.
  „ Hamson, F.
  „ Hanna, A. M. G.
  „ Haag, H. F.
  „ Hall, A. W.
✣Cpl. Harrison. H.
Pte. Hardisty, W.
  „ Hannant, G.
L.-Cpl. Hardy, W.
Pte. Handel, T.
  „ Hardisty, E. H. L.
✣ „ Hawkins, H. V.
  „ Harrington, F. K.
  „ Hammond, C. C.
Cpl. Hamburger, S.
✣Pte. Halliday, J. F.
✣ „ Harrison, A.
  „ Haslett, W. A.
✣ „ Handley, J. A.
  „ Hassen, V. G.
✣ „ Hallet, J.
  „ Hart, A. C.
  „ Harley, J. H.
  „ Harrison, G. C.

HISTORY OF 38th BATTALION, A.I.F. 99

L.-Cpl. Helms, P. J.
Cpl. Hession, R.
Sgt. Heslin, P.
✤Pte. Henry, R. A.
„ Henderson, A. H.
.. Henderson, R. S
✤ „ Healey, G. C.
„ Henderson, E. G.
✤ „ Heathcote, R. J.
✤ „ Heathcote, G. W.
L.-Cpl. Herring, L. H.
Pte. Helyar, A. J.
L.Cpl. Heyen, L.
Pte. Henderson, A. G. H.
„ Hegarty, D.
„ Herbert, P. T.
L.-Cpl. Hedgcock, E. E.
Pte. Healey, F. B.
„ Healy, S. T.
„ Hewett, J.
✤ „ Hepworth, G. J.
„ Heffernan, G. A.
Sgt. Heaney, J. R.
Pte. Hedger, A. W.
„ Henderson, A. I.
„ Henstridge, C. H. H.
Sgt. Hillerman, W. E.
Pte. Hill, A. W.
Sgt. Hick, H. B.
Pte. Hills, F. C.
L.-Cpl. Hilson, T. R.
Pte. Hildebrant, L. W.
„ Hirst, E. C.
„ Hickey, H. W.
Sgt. Hickey, L. R. P.
Pte. Hinten, D. C.
„ Hill, R. J.
✤ „ Hirth, A. S.
✤ „ Hislop, J. A.
„ Hill, L. A.
Cpl. Hirth. L. C.
Pte. Hooke, T. E.
„ Holmes, C. B.
„ Hobson. W. R.
✤ „ Hogan, M.
„ Howard, G. H.
„ Hook, W. A.
„ Hotchkins, W.
✤ „ Hosking, A. A.
„ Hollingsworth, A.
„ Holt, W. A.
✤Cpl. Hodgson, J. P.
Pte. Houghton, T.
„ Honeyman, D. C.
„ Hooper, G. H.
L.-Cpl. Hough, A. E. L.
Pte. Hocking, D.

Cpl. Horsey, E. L.
Pte. Hobbs, E.
✤Sgt. Howe, D. F.
Cpl. Homden, J. W. J.
Pte. Housden, W. E.
„ Hogg, A.
„ Howship, F. R.
Sgt. Holloway, E. H.
Pte. Hogan, E. H.
„ Hodgson, J. C.
✤ „ Holman, H. R.
„ Hogan, W. J.
✤ „ Hoffmeyer, N. J. W.
„ Hope, W.
„ Holmes, T.
„ Holmes, E. P.
L.-Cpl. Hodgens, T. V.
L.-Cpl. Holland, R. L.
✤Sgt. Howell, N. R.
Sgt. Hogan, W. J.
Pte. Hocking, A. J.
✤ „ Holmes C. J.
✤ „ Hole, H.
„ Hosking, J. V.
„ Holt, G.
„ Humrick, J.
✤Cpl. Hutchinson, W.
Sgt. Hutt, A. E.
Pte. Humphreys, G.
L.-Cpl. Hulme, F. W.
Sgt. Humphries, H. W.
Pte. Hultgren, F. H.
„ Hutchins, S. E.
L.-Sgt. Huggins, P. L.
Pte. Hudson, F. J.
„ Hutton, G.
„ Hutchinson, S.
„ Hull, D. T.
Sgt. Humffray, A. E.
Pte. Hullen, H.
„ Hull, O.
„ Hunter, P. H.
Dvr. Hutcheson, J.
✤Pte. Hudson, H.
„ Hutchinson, F.
✤ „ Huxley, A. J.
„ Hynes, J. E.
✤ „ Hyatt, G. J.
„ Hyde, E. T.
„ Hynes, F. E.
✤Cpl. Ihins, H. A.
Pte. Innes, C. R.
L.-Cpl. Ingleton, R. A.
Pte. Irwin, C. E.
✤ „ Irish, H. O.
✤L.-Sgt. Issell, S. G.
Pte. Ives, A.

✤Pte. Jasper, E.
Cpl. James, E. H.
✤Pte. Jager, A. F.
„ Jackson, R. J.
„ Jackson, A. R.
L.-Cpl. James, E. M.
Pte. James, W. H.
„ Jansen, W.
„ Jackson, M. A.
„ Jackson, D.
„ James, J. R.
„ Jacjung, L. L.
„ Jeffs, L.
✤„ Jennings, F. L.
„ Jeal, S. N.
✤„ Jennings, R.
✤„ Jenkins, A. E.
„ Jeanes, H. T.
L.-Cpl. Jenkins, E. W.
Pte. Jeffrey, T.
„ Jerrems, H. H.
„ Jenson, E. H.
„ Jeffrey, A. P.
„ Jephcott, T. C.
„ Jephson, P. W.
„ Jones, E. M.
„ Jones, A. A. L. B.
✤„ Johnson, H. A.
„ Johnson, J. A.
✤„ Johnson, A.
„ Jones, E. A. C.
„ Johns, T. H.
„ Joiner, W. E.
„ Johnston, R. J.
„ Johnson, C. A. G.
✤„ Joyce, S. J. F.
Sgt. Joseph, H. W.
Pte. Johnston, A.
L.-Cpl. Johns, A. A.
Pte. Jones, E. V.
„ Jones, W. L.
Cpl. Johansen, C.
Pte. Johnston, W. E.
„ Joiner, A. H.
„ Jones, W.
„ Johnstone, J.
✤Cpl. Jorgenson, C.
Pte. Jolme, J. P.
„ Johnstone, R. E.
„ Johnston, H. F. V.
„ Johnston, R. S.
„ Joseph, F. R.
„ Jones, J. M.
„ Johns, A.
„ Judd, J. E.
✤„ Jude, G. C.
„ Kavanagh, W. B.

✤Pte. Kay, L.
L.-Cpl. Kairn, J. A.
Pte. Kasch, J. F.
„ Kane, H. J.
✤Cpl. Kevan, R. L.
Pte. Kerr, J.
„ Kerwin, W. J.
„ Kerwin, S. C.
„ Kelly, F. D.
„ Kelly, P.
„ Keys, J. C.
„ Kessel, W. H.
Dvr. Keogh, E. D.
Pte. Kellow, W. J.
„ Kerr-Nelson, G.
„ Keegan, R. E.
„ Kirkland, E. E.
„ Kennedy, H. B.
Sgt. King, J. H. S.
✤Pte. King, A. R.
L.-Cpl. King, C. A. C.
✤Pte. Kirsch, V. R.
✤„ King, H. G.
„ Kirby, J.
„ Kidman, S. J.
„ Keil, C. H.
„ Kerwood, G. S.
„ King, H. A.
„ Kenworthy, H. A.
„ Keast, T. W. C.
„ Kemp, C. H.
„ Kerr, E.
Sgt. Kelly, R. B.
Pte. Kemp, F. L.
„ Kelly, F.
„ Kellet, J. F.
✤„ Knight, J. F.
„ Knuckey, A. E.
L.-Cpl. Knuckey, F. W.
✤Pte. Knight, R. H.
„ Knox, W. A.
„ Knowles, E. S.
„ Knight, A. H.
„ Knight, W.
„ Krake, P. W.
„ Kreig, W.
✤Cpl. Kurrle, H. G.
Pte. Kurtzman, R. V.
✤„ Langley, H. A.
„ Langley, R. S.
✤L.-Cpl. Lawler, F. M.
Pte. Lawler, J. E.
Dvr. Lacey, T. A.
L.-Cpl. Landells, A. W.
L.-Cpl. Laurie, D. P.
Pte. Laurie, J. E.
„ Lay, F. A.

Pte. Langdon, L. A.
„ Lacey, T. W.
„ Larcombe, E. L.
✢„ Lawson, A. B. L.
„ Lansell, C. S.
✢„ Langtry, W. M.
Cpl. Ladd, W. H.
Pte. Lazarus, W.
„ Layland, F. T.
„ Lancaster, J. W.
„ Layland, B. J.
L.-Cpl. Langgaard, N.
Pte. Lacey, T.
„ Lavery, B. P.
„ Laby, C. R.
„ Lawford, R. S.
„ Lambert, F.
„ Large, R. J.
„ Lawson, R.
„ Lawes, A. E.
„ Larsen, M. T.
Cpl. Ladlow, A.
✢Pte. Ladlow, O. H.
„ Langholtz, F. A.
„ Lawrey, B. K.
„ Lamont, F. W.
Sgt. Landon, W.
Pte. Leach, G.
„ Leys, G. S.
„ Lewton, E. C.
„ Leonard, T. J.
✢„ Ledwidge, W. H.
„ Le Conte, H. J. W.
„ Legg, L. J.
„ Leeson, A. J.
✢„ Lencke, E. B.
„ Lester, E. R.
L.-Cpl. Leslie, J.
„ Le Carle, C. J.
„ Leahy, T. D.
„ Leigh, A. F.
„ Leverington. L. H.
„ Leaver, E. T.
L.-Cpl. Lewis, J. C.
Pte. Lear, H. A.
„ Lewis, R. C.
L.-Cpl. Lever, H.
Pte. Lee, W. S.
„ Leach, R. W.
„ Lewis, W. L.
L.-Cpl. Lees, J. A.
Sgt. Lehmann, F. M.
Pte. Linden, A. J.
„ Lindrea, W. J.
„ Linnett, F. G.
„ Lillyst, C. L.
„ Lines, J. S.

Pte. Linsell, P.
✢„ Lobb, W. J.
„ Loam, A. S.
„ Lonsdale, F. L.
Sgt. Lockett, J. H.
Pte. Lowe, A. C. L.
✢„ Loader, G. A.
„ Lonsdale, R.
„ Lock, H.
Cpl. Looney, J. J.
Sgt. Long, N. B.
Pte. Lofts, A.
✢„ Lock, F.
Sgt. Lonsdale, H.
„ Lorimer, H.
✢Pte. Luecke, E. B.
Sgt. Lundgreen, J.
R.S.M. Lucas, W. F.
Pte. Lund, H. B.
Cpl. Luxon, R. H.
Pte. Lucas, J. S. B.
„ Lucas, R. J. B.
„ Pte. Lucas, J. N.
„ Luke, J. H.
✢„ Lydon, W. V.
✢„ Lynch, Geo. H.
„ Lynch, A. P.
„ Lynn, J. L.
Pte. Manning, L. J.
„ Marshall, S. J.
„ Matthews, R. E.
„ Marks, S. R.
✢L.-Cpl. Maynard, G. M.
Pte. Manallack, P. L.
„ Malcolm, C. W.
L.-Cpl. Marlow, P. P.
✢Pte. Marlow, A. W.
„ Maddern, F.
✢Sgt. Marlow, C. E.
Pte. Manning, W. A.
„ Marriott, W. E.
„ Manser, G. P.
„ Martin, R. W.
✢„ Martin, B. W.
✢„ Marra, H. E.
✢Cpl. Manning, W. R.
Pte. Martin, W. H.
L.-Sgt. Mayo, E. D.
Pte. Mannix, J. J.
✢„ Marion, W. S.
✢„ Matheson, R. L.
„ MacQueen, A. C.
✢„ Malkin, C. W.
✢„ Merrett, H. T.
„ Meagher, N. B.
✢„ Meredith, R. S.
„ Mew, B.

Pte. Matheson, J.
 „ Martin, S. G.
 „ Martin, J. C.
 „ Maisey, G. G. C.
✤„ Matson, J. H.
 „ Mahoney, A. B.
 „ Martin, P. E.
 „ Mayne, L.
 „ Marshall, W. C.
 „ Macreadie, W.
Sgt. Madill, A. E.
Sgt. Marrett, F. W. P.
Pte. Makepeace, E. G.
 „ Maloney, W. B.
Sgt. Matchan, W. J.
Pte. Martin, H.
 „ Matthews, A. M. J.
✤„ Maggs, F. G.
 „ MacLean, E. G.
Cpl. Mack, R. A.
✤Pte. Manning, W. J.
 „ Marassovich, M. Y. N.
✤„ Marshall, B. C.
 „ Mason, W. T.
✤„ Masters, A. E.
 „ Maher, W. J.
 „ Mason, T. G.
✤„ Maitland, J. A.
 „ Maslin, S. F.
 „ Marks, P.
 „ Maddocks, A. J.
L.-Cpl. Mayberry, G. C.
✤Pte. Meyerink, J. J.
 „ Meyer, W. H.
 „ Meadows, J.
 „ Meyer, J. E.
 „ Meredith, W. A.
 „ Meere, R. W.
Sgt. Meredith, J. V.
Pte. Merry, A. E.
✤„ Meldrum, L. R.
 „ Meagher, M. B.
 „ Meagher, G.
 „ Mitchell, V.
✤„ Millar, A. I.
 „ Mitchell, M. V.
 „ Mitchem, C. C.
Q.M.S. Miller, I. P.
Pte. Miller, Joseph.
✤„ Miller, John.
Sgt. Mills, G.
Pte. Mills, A.
✤„ Mills, H. S.
L.-Cpl. Mills, C. A.
Pte. Middleton, H. G.
✤„ Midolo, M. J.
✤„ Miller, S. O.

Pte. Mills, E.
 „ Minnitt, F.
 „ Milligan, R. J.
 „ Miller, E.
 „ Milne, H. E.
 „ Miller, G.
L.-Cpl. Mitchell, S. J.
Pte. Miller, H. A.
Cpl. Mills, E.
Pte. Mitchell, J. P.
 „ Miller, H.
✤„ Mitchell, J. F.
 „ Mitchell, P. D.
 „ Mitchell, L. F.
Cpl. Morgan, B. N.
✤Pte. Moore, G. W.
 „ Morgan, G. W.
 „ Moore, G. W. E.
✤„ Moore, F. L.
✤„ Mossop, G.
 „ Mowat, W. P.
Cpl. Moore, R.
Pte. Moore, C. L.
 „ Moore, N. D.
Cpl. Morrissey, J. J.
L.-Cpl. Morrison, A.
Pte. Mowbray, J.
✤„ Morrow, H. J.
 „ Mongan, W.
 „ Moore, W. J.
 „ Morrison, C. J.
 „ Morrison, D. H.
✤„ Moore, G.
 „ Morrissey, M. J.
 „ Moult, F. J.
 „ Moor, A. S.
 „ Moore-Robinson,
 „ Monaghan, W.
L.-Cpl. Moon, F. H. A.
Pte. Mooney, G. P.
✤„ Morris, J.
.. Moss, E. N.
L.-Cpl. Moss, W. S.
Pte. Montiford, J. W.
 „ Murray, K.
Sgt. Murray, R.
Sgt. Mulquiny, E.
✤„ Murphy, J. T.
Cpl. Murphy, T. L.
Pte. Munche, J.
✤„ Murdoch, G.
✤„ Munday, J. R.
 „ Mullen, J. T.
 „ Murray, R. T.
 „ Murray, J.
L.-Cpl. Munro, K. A. R.
Pte. Muir, W. N.

Pte. Murphy, A.
❋L.-Cpl. Myers, J. L. K.
Pte. Myers, W. H.
L.-Cpl. McAuley, A. F.
Pte. McAleer, C.
" McAleese, B.
" McAulliffe, G. C.
Dvr. McBean, J. R.
Sgt. McCallum, H.
Pte. McCormick, T. J.
Dvr. McCorkell, S. J. T.
Pte. McClure, R. G.
L.-Cpl. McClure, G. W.
❋Pte. McClure, T. A.
" McCausland, L. H.
" McCarthy, E.
" McCarthy, J. L.
" McCormack, S.
❋" McCormack, A.
" McCuspie, P.
" McCrea, D. A.
" McCoy, F. C.
❋" McCullock, G.
" McClure, A.
" McCormack, J. J.
L.-Sgt. McCormick, N. J.
Pte. McCartney, W. G.
" McCutcheon, W. F.
L.-Cpl. McDonald, J. R.
❋Pte. McDowell, J.
❋Cpl. McDonald, T. A.
Sgt. McDonald, N. A.
Cpl. McDonald, A. C.
Pte. McDonald, C. R.
" McDermott, D. J.
" McDonald, A.
" McDougall, D.
❋" McDonald, J.
" McDonald, L.
❋" McDonald, G. L.
Cpl. McDonald, J. A.
Pte. McDonald. E. R.
" McDonald, R.
" McDermott, E. J.
Cpl. McDonald, S. G.
Pte. McDonald, A. E.
❋" McDonald, H.
L.-Cpl. McDonald, E. H.
Pte. McDonald, J. W. S.
Sgt. McElroy, J. W.
❋Pte. McEwan, W.
" McFadyen, J. A.
❋" McFarlane, R. A.
" McGarvie, J. B.
" McGregor, J.
" McGrice, R. R.
" McGrady, J.

Pte. McGann, T. J.
" McGrath, W.
" McGuiness, T.
" McGladdery, G.
" McGregor, D. T.
❋" McGlashan, A.
" McGinley, E.
Sgt. McInnes, J. W.
❋Pte. McInnes, A. A.
" McIntyre, E.
" McIvor, P.
" McIvor, D.
" McIntosh, J.
" McIntyre, R. M.
" McKay, J.
" McKenzie, D. A.
Sgt. McKinnon. W. S.
Pte. McKee, W. E.
" McKenzie, R. M.
Sgt. McKenzie, D. W.
Pte. McKenzie, W.
" McKenna, H.
❋" McKenzie, P. G.
" McKelvie, A. H.
L.-Cpl. McKenzie, P.
Pte. McKenzie, A.
" McLean, L. H.
" McLean, G.
Cpl. McLeod, J.
Pte. McLeod, W. E.
❋" McLean, H. A.
" McLennan, N. W.
Cpl. McLeod, C. W.
❋Pte. McLaughlan, O.
" McLaughlan, J.
" McLean, O. J.
" McLean, G. L.
" McLachlan, J. H.
" McLachlan, J.
" McLaren, J. L.
L.-Cpl. McMaster, A. F.
Pte. McMaster, A.
" McMaster, A. E.
" McMaster, E.
❋" McMurtrie, J.
❋" McMurtrie, F. A.
" McManus, T. W.
" McMillan, W.
Sgt. McNeil, J. D.
L.-Cpl. McNiven, D.
Pte. McNeil, R.
" McNulty, W. R.
" McNamara, J. V.
" McPherson, M.
❋" McPherson, W. B.
" McPherson, D.
Cpl. McPhee, A.

Pte. McPhee, J.
 ,, McPherson, S. G.
 ,, McPherson, A.
 ,, McQueen, R. A.
L.-Cpl. McRae, W. G.
✤Pte. McRae, M.
L.-Cpl. McTaggart, C. A.
Sgt. McTaggart, J.
Pte. McVicar. A. A..
 ,, McWalkaton, K. W.
 ,, Nash, A. C. D.
✤Cpl. Nathan, E. W.
L.-Cpl. Newell, W. J. L.
Pte. Neilson, R. S.
 ,, Nelson, A.
✤,, Nelson, J. H.
✤,, Needham, W. G.
 ,, Newandt, F. C.
✤L.-Cpl. Newton, W. G.
Pte. Newton, C. E.
✤,, Neighbour, W. J.
 ,, Nelson, A. B.
 ,, Nelson, B. I.
C.S.M. Newton, A. G.
Pte. Neill, J.
 ,, Negro, C. A.
 ,, Nieman, W.
R.Q.M.S. Nicholl, J. W. A.
Pte. Nihill, J. J.
✤,, Nihill, M. J.
Sgt. Nihill, P. L.
✤Pte. Nield, W. J.
 ,, Nicholson, H.
 ,, Nicholson, J. D.
 ,, Nicholls, E. A. V.
✤,, Nicholes, G.
L.-Cpl. Nicoll, J.
Pte. Nixon. H.
 ,, Nichols, J. W.
 ,, North, E. A.
 ,, Nolan, E. J.
 ,, Nowlan, E. J.
✤Cpl. Norton, C. R. B.
Pte. Noble, H. V.
 ,, Nolan, H. C.
 ,, Norris, A.
 ,, Noble, W. J.
 ,, Noonan, J.
 ,, Nyblom, F. A.
 ,, Oakley, A. E.
 ,, O'Brien, M. E.
 ,, O'Brien, M. J.
 ,, O'Brien, N. J.
 ,, O'Brien, C. E.
✤,, O'Connor, J. J.
L.-Cpl. Odlum, R. H.
˙Pte. O'Dea, J. J.

Pte. O'Donoghue, A.
 ,, O'Donnell, E. T.
 ,, Offerman, R. W.
✤,, Ogden, G. M.
 ,, Ohlsen, W. P.
Cpl. Oliver, E. A.
✤L.-Cpl. Oliver, H. F.
Sgt. Onley, R. E.
✤Sgt. Onians, N. G.
✤Pte. O'Neill, R. F.
 ,, Opie, J. J
✤,, Onpy W. E.
 ,, Cram, D.
Cpl. O Shea, J. C
Pte. O'Shea, J.
 ,, Osgood, H. R.
 ,, Osgood, B. B.
✤Cpl. O'Shannessy, M. T.
✤Pte. O'Sullivan, J. H. T.
 ,, Ostrom, A. C.
✤,, Ott, P. C.
 ,, O'Toole, T. J.
 ,, Overall, W. H. T.
 ,, Owens, P.
 ,, Owens, A. L.
✤,, Owen, A. V.
 ,, Owen J.
 ,, Oxenham, S. H.
Sgt. Patterson, H. W.
Sgt. Palk, A.
 ,, Pascoe, J. T.
✤Pte. Pay, C.
✤L.-Sgt. Pankhurst, H.
Pte. Patterson, B.
 ,, Patterson, G.
✤,, Pate, W. C. H.
 ,, Parker, W. H.
 ,, Parker, S. A.
 ,, Passmore, W. F.
 ,, Parfett, A. J.
 ,, Parsons, R.
 ,, Parsons, T. C.
Cpl. Paton, R. W.
Pte. Patterson, W. J.
✤,, Park, J. J.
 ,, Palmer, J. J.
 ,, Pasque, E. W.
 ,, Palmer, L.
✤,, Pack, A.
 ,, Parsons, H. R.
✤,, Page, R. L.
 ,, Parsons, R. P.
 ,, Patterson, C. A.
✤Cpl. Paterson, R.
L.-Cpl. Palmer, H. A.
 ,, Parnall, F.
✤Pte. Page, W. R.

HISTORY OF 38th BATTALION, A.I.F. 105

Pte. Partington, E.
" Parkinson, H. W.
L.-Cpl. Pearce, J. A. D.
Pte. Peatty, A. W.
" Penman, D.
L.-Cpl. Peck, A.
L.Cpl. Petherick, A. V.
L.-Cpl. Perry, F. J.
Pte. Petterson, P. E.
" Percy, O. W.
" Perry, L. S.
❋ " Perrett, E.
,. Pettingill, C. R.
L.-Cpl. Penny, F. C.
Pte. Petter, W.
" Peeks, T. H.
❋ " Peacock, D.
" Pearce, A.
" Peken, E. J.
Sgt. Pegler, A. E.
Pte. Pfau, M.
" Phillips, R. J.
" Phillips, F. E.
❋ " Phayer, R. M.
Q.M.S. Phillips, L. S.
❋Pte. Pinch, W. J.
Cpl. Piggott, E.
" Pinnell, L. W.
Sgt. Piggott, J. J.
Pte. Piggott, G.
" Pike, J. W.
L.-Cpl. Pippin, H.
Pte. Pilling, D. C.
" Plate, A. C.
" Plush, A. H. G.
Cpl. Plim, J.
Pte. Powell, W. E. G.
" Porter, C. J.
❋ " Powell, A. B.
" Potter, S. M.
.. Poppleton, A.
❋ " Powell, W. G.
" Pope, E. E. V.
" Pte. Pocock, J. S.
.. Pockett, A. H.
" Poppins, E. T.
L.-Cpl. Price, G. F.
Pte. Price, G. F.
❋L.-Cpl. Pryse, D.
Pte. Pringle, D.
,. Prowse, G. S.
" Pritchard, L. W.
❋ ., Prince, A.
Sgt. Preston, H. F.
Pte. Prange, F. H.
L.-Cpl. Purcell, G. V.
Pte. Pugh, V. A.

Pte. Purdy, A. R.
" Pummeroy, J.
" Puls, B. A.
" Pyke, W. G.
" Pyers, G.
" Pyers, L.
Sgt. Quinn, R. A.
Pte. Qualey, J.
C.Q.M.S. Quinton, B. J.
Pte. Quilty, J. P.
" Quinlan, T. J.
" Quirk, J.
" Quin, S. T.
❋ " Radnell, C. V.
❋ " Rawlings, T. H.
L.-Cpl. Radnell, H. W.
Sgt. Raybould, A. J. B.
Pte. Radoslovich, J.
" Ranson, J. G.
" Rawlings, F.
" Randle, T.
Cpl. Rankin, F. G.
Pte. Ray, G. S.
L.-Sgt. Rangecroft, H. C.
Pte. Radford, A.
❋ " Rasmussen, J. R.
❋ " Radford, E.
❋ " Reid, A.
,. Revill, V. H.
" Reddie, E. A.
Cpl. Reid, J.
Pte. Rees, J. S.
❋ " Reville, F. W.
" Reed, V.
❋Sgt. Read, C. C.
Pte. Reid, J.
" Redman, J. H.
Cpl. Redman, F. H.
Pte. Reilly, T. E.
" Reigner, H. R.
" Read, A. H.
,. Read, H.
Cpl. Reid, C. J.
Pte. Read, J. R.
Cpl. Rhodes, J.
Pte. Rhodes, J. A.
,. Rhodes, A. E.
" Rimes, P. P.
❋ " Rich, F. P.
❋L.-Cpl. Riddock, W. T.
❋Pte. Richardson, E. J.
" Richie, J. M.
" Rivett, W. H.
Cpl. Rigby, S. B.
❋L.-Cpl. Risbey, G. S.
Pte. Richards, T. G.
❋ " Ridgway, G. E.

Pte. Rich, W. G.
" Rimmer, R.
" Ride, L. T.
✽ " Rickard, A.
" Richardson, J. B.
✽ " Rippin, A.
" Rickard, W. H.
✽ " Richards, D. T.
" Riley, M. E.
✽ " Robertson, J.
" Robinson, J. W.
✽ " Robinson, A. R.
" Robinson, S. B.
" Ross, R. G.
" Roberts, J. J.
" Robertson, W.
✽ " Roxburgh, J.
✽Pte Rooney, M.
✽ " Roger, A. S.
" Ross, W. H.
" Rodgers, A. A.
" Robertson, D. K.
L.-Cpl. Roberts, P. A.
Pte. Roberts, S. D.
" Robertson, D. A.
Sgt. Rowling, W. L.
Pte. Roberts, W. J.
" Rowe, P. B.
" Robertson, E. R.
✽L.-Cpl. Routley, C. T.
Sgt. Roake, L. E.
Sgt. Rowe, H. M.
✽Pte. Rohde, H. W.
" Rowe, S.
" Rooney, C. E.
" Robinson, R.
L.-Sgt. Robson, G. H. E.
Pte. Rohan, J.
Sgt. Ross, H. M.
L.-Cpl. Rogers, J. M.
Sgt. Roberts, H.
Pte. Rowlands, W.
Cpl. Robertson, J.
Pte. Rowe, G. R.
Sgt. Rook, J.
Pte. Rolls, R.
" Rodgers, C. N.
" Robinson, R. H.
" Rowe, R. R.
✽ " Roberts, T. S.
✽Sgt. Ross, R. H.
✽Pte. Robertson, A.
Sgt. Runting, A.
Pte. Russell, W. W.
Sgt. Runge, F. H.
✽R.S.M. Rust, A. E.
✽Pte. Rudolph, O. G.

Pte. Rumble, H. S.
" Russell, E. L.
" Ryan, M.
" Ryan, A.
" Ryan, J. T.
✽ " Ryan, A. C. L.
" Ryan, L. T.
" Savage, A.
L.-Cpl. Savage, R. A.
Pte. Saunders, P. F.
" Satchell, L. M.
" Samuel, R.
" Sargent, W. R.
" Sands, W. J.
" Sawyer, C. P.
" Sargeant, S. C.
" Scott, N.
" Scammell, A. G.
✽ " Scown, J.
✽ " Scott, P. J.
" Scroope, H. L.
" Schmidt, C. B.
Sgt. Scoberg, J. H.
✽Pte. Scott, J. J.
Pte. Scott, E. E.
" Scrace. G. J.
" Scott, D.
✽ " Schunke, W. A.
✽ " Scott, J. T.
" Scott, A.
" Scott, R. S.
" Scott, S. W.
" Scane, B. S. F.
" Sexton, J. P.
" Seymour, C. E.
" Semple, H. F.
" Seider, T. F.
" Sercombe, F. S.
✽Cpl. Semmens, H. J.
Pte. Seymour, G. V.
" Seymour, F.
Cpl. Shacklock, H.
L.-Cpl. Shout, A. J.
Pte. Sharpland, A. H.
" Shone, W. H.
" Shaw, H.
✽ " Sheridan, R. A.
" Shepherd, W. J.
" Shelly, D.
Sgt. Shacklock, C. J.
Pte. Shepherd, A.
✽Cpl. Sheldrick, R. A.
C.S.M. Sharp, J. H.
Sgt. Shuttlewood, J. A.
Pte. Shaw, A. E.
" Sheringham, C.
Cpl. Shugg, W.

Pte. Sheppard, A. W.
„ Shadforth, G. E. T.
„ Shields, A.
✲ „ Shearwood, W. C.
✲L.-Cpl. Shone, C.
Pte. Shaw, C. V.
„ Shaw, B.
C.Q.M.S. Shelton, H. W.
L.-Cpl. Shillinglaw, E. S.
Pte. Sharp, M.
„ Shaw, A. G.
✲ „ Sheahan, H.
„ Simms, F.
✲ „ Siler, E. J.
Sgt. Siden, O. A.
✲Pte. Sims, A.
L.-Cpl. Sinclair, R. B.
Pte. Sinclair, A. J.
„ Simons, W. E.
„ Simms, F. N.
„ Simms, W. E.
„ Simon, J. H.
„ Sinclair, S. A.
„ Simpson, W.
„ Simmons, J.
„ Sim, P. T.
„ Silsby, E. B.
„ Simmonds, J.
„ Sillitoe, R. J.
„ Sinclair, A.
„ Skilbeck, T.
„ Slater, W.
„ Slatter, W. T.
„ Slatter, J. G.
„ Slade, M. J.
„ Smith, L. C.
Dvr. Smith, D.
✲Pte. Smith, W. C.
Cpl. Smith, E.
Pte. Smith, H. H.
„ Smith, L. C.
„ Smith, W. J.
„ Smith, E. E.
„ Smith, S. T.
„ Smith, J.
„ Smith, C.
„ Smith, H. F.
✲ „ Smith, J. W.
„ Smith, S. R.
„ Smith, C. H.
„ Smith, H. T.
„ Smith, R. F.
✲ „ Smith, L.
L.-Cpl. Smith, H.
Sgt. Smith, W. D.
Pte. Smith, R. A.
„ Smith, J.

Pte. Smith, A. L.
L.-Cpl. Smith, E. A. G.
Pte. Smith, W. B.
✲ „ Smith, H. K.
„ Smith, T. R.
„ Smyth, G. P.
✲ „ Smythe, H. M.
„ Smart, W.
„ Snowden, J. J.
„ Snell, C. C.
„ Sorrell, W. J.
„ Spooner, A. S.
Sgt. Spencer, G.
Pte. Speers, L. J.
Pte. Spinks, T. S.
Sgt. Spry, W. P.
Pte. Spencer, A. A.
„ Spence, P. G.
„ Spalding, P. H.
Sgt. Strickland, L.
✲Pte. Stirling, W. J.
L.-Cpl. Strouss, A. F.
Pte. Stevens, E. W.
„ Stringer, F. D.
„ Stevens, H. J.
„ Stubbs, A.
„ Stratton, J.
✲ „ Sturman, W. H.
„ Stevens, W. T.
„ Steele, J. S.
Cpl. Stanbury, W. E.
Pte. Styles, H.
✲ „ Stephenson, E.
„ Stratford, A.
✲ „ Stockwell, A. J.
„ St. Leon, A.
„ Stoker, G.
✲ „ Stevens, J. T.
„ Stretton, E. G.
„ Stevenson, H.
✲L.-Cpl. Stammers, W. J.
Pte. Steele, J. A. P.
✲Cpl. Stevens, L. A.
Pte. Strachan, A. V.
„ Strachan, D. R.
„ Strachan, D. G.
„ Street, H.
„ Stephenson, J. C.
„ Street, W.
Cpl. Stanley, T.
Pte. Stringer, F. D.
„ Suhle, W. F.
✲ „ Sullivan, M. J.
Cpl. Sutton, H.
Cpl. Sullivan, M. T.
✲L.-Cpl. Sullivan, J. W. H.
✲Pte. Sullivan, E. D.

Pte. Sutherland, R. V.
 „   Suhle, W. F.
Sgt. Suggett, R. J.
Pte. Swadling, A. J.
 „   Swan, F. W.
 „   Swift, L. C.
 ,. Swainston, E. G.
L.-Cpl. Symonds, E. O.
Cpl. Symonds, A. O.
Pte. Sypott, H. Q.
Cpl. Symonds, A. O.
Pte. Syme, D. H.
 „   Symes, C. E.
 „   Symon, J. H.
 „   Syphers, A. E.
 „   Taylor, L. B.
 „   Taylor, C. H.
L.-Cpl. Taylor, J. E.
Pte. Taylor, G. H.
Sgt. Taylor, W. E.
❋Pte. Taylor, L. C.
 ., Taylor, L. J.
❋ „ Taylor, C.
❋ ., Taylor, S. V.
 .. Taylor, A. J.
 „   Taylor, G.
C.S.M. Taylor, A. J. C.
Pte. Taylor, P. H.
 „   Taylor, A. E.
 „   Taylor, L. B.
❋ ., Taylor, W. E.
 „   Taylor, F. E.
 ,. Taylor, H. R.
 „   Taylor, C. A.
 „   Talbot, C. R. A.
 ,. Tacey, A. E.
Sgt. Tate, G. J.
Pte. Teasdale, J. M.
❋Cpl. Teague, A. W.
Pte. Terry, S. W.
 „   Tevelein, G. J.
❋ ., Terry, L. B.
 ., Tedge, J. L.
❋ .. Tester, A. L.
❋ .. Teale, W.
 ,. Telfor, A. L.
 .. Teichelman, R. C.
❋ .. Thompson, H. H.
❋ .. Thompson, J. V.
 „   Thewlis, A.
 .. Thomas, W. E.
 ., Thomas, G. H.
 .. Thrum, M. H.
 .. Thompson, G. H.
 „   Thom, W.
C.S.M. Thompson, I. J.
Pte. Thompson, C. G.

Pte. Thomas, C. Mc.
 „   Thrum, G. H.
 „   Thompson, R.
 „   Thomson, A.
 „   Thompson, W. E.
 „   Thompson, V. G.
❋ „ Thompson, R.
 „   Thompson, J. A.
 „   Thwaites, W. A. A.
 „   Tierny, F. R.
Sgt. Tilley, G. E.
Pte. Tippett, C.
 „   Tillig, C. G.
 „   Tiller, W. A.
❋L.-Cpl. Todd, A. J.
Pte. Toll, S. H. V.
 ,. Towers, T.
 „   Tough, J.
 „   Toohey, E. L.
❋ „ Townsend, D. L.
❋ ,. Trew, W.
Sgt. Trebilcock, F. E.
❋Pte. Treloar, J. H.
 ,. Trengrove, F. W.
L.-Cpl. Treacy, J. W.
❋Pte. Treloar, A. J.
 „   Trenter, A. T.
❋ ,. Tracey, E.
 „   Trigg, A.
 .. Triggs, R. W.
L.-Sgt. Trevaskis, W. J.
Pte. Trevaskis, J. M.
 „   Tranter, B.D.
 ,. Tranter, A. M. E.
 „   Trueman, F.
 .. Tracey, J.
L.-Cpl. Tutor, H. W. H.
Pte. Turner, R. J.
 ,. Turner, F.
 ., Tuckwell, J.
 „   Turney, G. R.
 „   Turley, P.
 „   Turnbull, E. D.
❋ .. Turnour, A. W.
❋Sgt. Tuckfield, H. R.
Pte. Turner, E. S. G.
 ,. Tuttle, T. J. V.
 „   Tucker, E. H. V.
 „   Turnbull, T. A.
❋L.-Cpl. Twomey, J. R.
Pte. Twomey, W. G.
 ,, Tyler, J.
 .. Tyers, W. A.
 „   Tyrrell, W. T.
 .. Uchtman, A.
 .. Umbers, E. C.
 „   Unsworth, J. J.

※Pte. Unger, R. L.
„ Unwin, A. H.
Cpl. Ure, D. T.
※L.-Cpl. Urquhart, W.
Pte. Vagg, F.
Cpl. Vale, F. S.
Pte. Vaughan, A. J.
„ Verso, A. J. J.
L.-Cpl. Verlin, C. M. S.
Pte. Vearing, E. J.
„ Venn, F. J.
„ Vickerman, W. T.
※„ Vivian, E. F.
„ Virtue, V. W.
※„ Voneinem, H. E.
„ Ward, C. E.
※R.Q.M.S. Watt, T. O.
※Pte. Waterhouse, F. E.
Sgt. Waterston, R. A.
Sgt. Wallace, C. T.
※„ Wallis, A. W.
Pte. Watson, W. H.
„ Waite, G. O.
„ Walters, B. G.
„ Watson, E.
„ Walker, A.
„ Watt, R.
. „ Warren, T. F.
※„ Walker, R. B.
L.-Cpl. Watson, A. V.
Pte. Waugh, A. D.
„ Walsh, J. H.
※„ Walsh, J.
※„ Walsh, E. J.
※Sgt. Walsh, J. F.
Pte. Ward, T. J.
„ Watts, J. N.
„ Watson, W. G.
※„ Warner, A. G.
„ Watts, R. A.
„ Waterland, H.
„ Wallis, W. J.
※„ Warne, V. E.
„ Wareham, A.
„ Waltho, W. G.
„ Ward, M.
„ Walker, R. J.
„ Watson, A. H.
„ Ward, G. E.
※„ Warwick, J. D.
„ Walsh, J.
„ Walsh, J. P.
Cpl. Wallace, J.
„ Ward, C. E.
Pte. Wallace, H. W.
L.-Cpl. Watt, D. A.
Sgt. Walker, O. H.

L.-Cpl. Wattz, J. H.
Pte. Watson, W. C.
„ Waye, H. R. M.
„ Ward, A. E.
„ Westland, C. L.
„ Wescombe, T. W. C.
※„ Wearne, J. S.
„ West, H. H.
„ Westwood, W. J.
※„ Welch, W. J.
Cpl. Webster, S.
„ Weston, W.
※„ Westgarth, F. A.
※„ Weaver, R.
„ Westgarth, W. J.
„ Westerberg, E. A.
※„ Westley, E. J.
„ Werner, A. R.
※„ Weir, F. W.
„ Werner, W. H.
„ Webb, L. J.
„ Westblade, J. H.
„ Webb, S. T.
„ Westwood, J. S.
„ Westwood, R.
„ Wearne, W. A.
Cpl. White, W. L.
※Pte. Whiteside, J.
※L.-Cpl. Whitemore, E. A.
Pte. Whaley, W.
※Sgt. Whitelaw, F.
Cpl. White, H. B.
Pte. White, J. J.
„ Whitfield, F. T.
„ Wheeldon, H. G.
„ White, F. L.
„ Whitton, A. J.
Cpl. Whipp, R. W.
Pte. White, A. J.
„ White, P. S.
„ Wheatley, J.
„ White, W.
„ Whyte, P. J.
„ Wheeler, F. J.
„ Wilson, G. L.
Sgt. Wilson, A. R. E.
※Pte. Wigg, C. E.
※„ Williams, J. O.
„ Williams, J. F.
„ Wilson, J.
Cpl. Willis, W. J.
Pte. Williams, E. T.
„ Willis, M. F.
„ Winstone, R. R.
L.-Cpl. Willoughby, J. T.
Pte. Winfield, V. A.
„ Wishart, H. S.

Pte. Williams, R.
 „ Wilson, L. N.
 „ Williams, J. N.
✿ „ Wilson, H. M.
 „ Wilton, G. L. D.
Cpl. Willis, R. A. P.
✿Pte. Wilds, S. J.
✿ „ Wilson, J. B.
 „ Wilson, W. G.
 „ Williams, H. T.
 „ Wilkie, G. M.
Sgt. Williams, E. W.
✿Pte. Wilson, J.
✿ „ Wilson, A. S.
 „ Wilson, G.
 „ Willis, J. H.
 „ Wilson, D. T.
✿ „ Wilkinson, E. R.
✿ „ Wilkie, G. R.
 „ Wilmot, A. G.
Dvr. Willetts, E. C.
 „ Wills, T. P.
Pte. Willingham, H. R.
 „ Williamson, T. H.
✿ „ Wise, W. M.
 „ Williamson, E. D.
Cpl. Wills, R.
✿Pte. Willis, S. F.
L.-Cpl. Willis, W. E.
✿Pte. Wishart, R. A.
 „ Windridge, H.
 „ Winstanley, T. W.
 „ Williams, T. G.
✿ „ Wilson, A. W.
✿ „ Williams, W. H.
✿ „ Wilkins, F.
 „ Wilson, D. I.
 „ Wilson, A. J.
 „ Wilson, R. T.
 „ Wilson, H.
 „ Wilson, H. A.

Sgt. Wilson, W. G.
Pte. Williams, J. G. A.
 „ Wishart, D. T. H.
 „ Williams, J. H. S.
✿ „ Willis, M.
 „ Wingate, J.
 „ Williams, C.
L.-Cpl. Wiseman, R. O. S.
Pte. Williams, T.
 „ Wilson, W. G.
✿ „ Worthy, P. W.
 „ Wood, J.
✿ „ Wood, R. A.
 „ Wood, G.
 „ Woodhouse, H. M.
 „ Wolstenholme, P. J.
 „ Wootan, E.
✿ „ Wouda, G.
L.-Cpl. Wormald, W. E.
Pte. Wood, W.
 „ Wood, G. L.
 „ Woods, E. A.
 „ Wright, S. G.
L.-Cpl. Wright, C. R.
Pte. Wright, O. D.
 „ Wright, J. K.
✿ „ Wundenberg, F. T.
✿ „ Wynniat, T. S. V.
✿Cpl. Yarra, A. J.
✿Pte. Yates, E. T.
 „ Yates, W. H.
 „ Young, A. G. L.
 „ Yole, A.
 „ Young, J. J.
 „ Youens, W. A.
 „ Young, C.
 „ Young, W. C.
✿ „ Young, G. F.
 „ Young, T.
 „ Zilles, G. S.

www.ingramcontent.com/pod-product-compliance
Lightning Source LLC
Chambersburg PA
CBHW032002080426
42735CB00007B/489